PRAISE FOR MONICA C. SMITH

This father-daughter tale reveals how the author's father taught her how to fight and survive in an unfiltered America. Born in the early 1940s, her father was thrown into a world where he had no choice but to fight in many different arenas, including the boxing ring and the courtroom. He instilled in her his unrelenting drive and will to win. As a result, she went through life with his priceless survival playbook at her side. She became a corporate commercial real estate (CRE) director and dealmaker overcoming adversity to manage billion-dollar real estate portfolios. She also walked the path of a CRE broker.

Based on true stories, join Monica as she narrates her father's lifelong quest for justice and how it impacted his parenting and subsequently her life. She will take readers on the powerful and poignant journeys of her and her father, covering decades from the 1940s through present day—from Northwest Indiana to New York City and points in between.

Long before the last page, readers will find themselves deeply contemplating their life journey and wishing they had the author and her father somewhere in their personal orbit.

Steel Victories will...

- Reveal the necessity of having Black fathers in the home and their impact on their children.
- Turbocharge you to never run from a fight for your dignity.
- Share secret weapons for navigating life's challenges.
- Give you a peek into the "secret society" of commercial real estate in Corporate America.
- Encourage you to face your faith.

STEEL VICTORIES
A FATHER-DAUGHTER SUCCESS STORY

MONICA C. SMITH

STEEL VICTORIES LLC

FOREWORD

I recently had the pleasure of reading *Steel Victories,* written by Monica C. Smith. This powerful and moving book tells the story of the author's father, a man who faced numerous challenges in his life but always managed to improvise, adapt, and overcome through sheer determination and resilience.

The author has a unique ability to capture her father's spirit, describing his struggles and triumphs in a way that is both honest and empathetic. She paints a vivid picture of a man who, despite facing adversity, never lost sight of his goals and always pushed forward.

What I found most striking about this book was the author's ability to convey the sense of empowerment that her father instilled in her. It's clear that she has been deeply influenced by his example and that his determination and perseverance has helped shape her into the person she is today.

I highly recommend *Steel Victories* to anyone looking for inspiration and motivation. This book is not only a tribute to an extraordinary man, but it also serves as a powerful reminder of the resilience and strength that exists within all of us. It will be especially empowering for African Americans and others who face challenges in their lives.

In short, this book is a must-read for anyone looking for a moving and inspiring story of a father and daughter and the lessons they learned together along the way.

David Wickenden

Publisher: Steel Victories LLC

Copyright © 2024 by Monica C. Smith

All rights reserved.

This work is based upon real events. Certain events, dialogue, and characters were created for the purposes of fictionalization.

No part of this publication may be reproduced, distributed, or transmitted in any form or by any means, including photocopying, recording, or other electronic or mechanical methods, without the prior written permission of the publisher, except as permitted by U.S. copyright law. For permission requests, please contact www.steelvictories.com or authormonicasmith@gmail.com.

Scriptures taken from the Holy Bible, New International Version®, NIV®. Copyright © 1973, 1978, 1984, 2011 by Biblica, Inc.™ Used by permission of Zondervan. All rights reserved worldwide. www.zondervan.com. The "NIV" and "New International Version" are trademarks registered in the United States Patent and Trademark Office by Biblica, Inc.™

Scripture quotations marked (NIrV) are taken from the Holy Bible, New International Reader's Version®, NIrV® Copyright © 1995, 1996, 1998, 2014 by Biblica, Inc.™ Used by permission of Zondervan. All rights reserved worldwide. www.zondervan.com. The "NIrV" and "New International Reader's Version" are trademarks registered in the United States Patent and Trademark Office by Biblica, Inc.™

Scripture quotations taken from the (NASB®) New American Standard Bible®, Copyright © 1960, 1971, 1977,1995, 2020 by The Lockman Foundation. Used by permission. All rights reserved. www.lockman.org.

Scripture quotations are from The ESV® Bible (The Holy Bible, English Standard Version®), copyright © 2001 by Crossway, a publishing ministry of Good News Publishers. Used by permission. All rights reserved.

Scripture quotations taken from the (NASB®) New American Standard Bible®, Copyright © 1960, 1971, 1977, 1995 by The Lockman Foundation. Used by permission. All rights reserved. www.lockman.org. –own property Leviticus 20

Scriptures marked KJV are taken from the KING JAMES VERSION (KJV): KING JAMES VERSION, public domain.

ISBN 979-8-9859432-0-7

Black and white photo on cover: credit to US Army

Torch Credit to WebHostingHub.com Glyphs – licensed OFL 1.1

Book Cover Design Inspired by: Monica C. Smith

Book Cover Artist: RAHIEM

I would like to dedicate this book to Jesus my savior and my mom and dad. I would also like to dedicate this book to my first best friend and first roommate and sister, Gabrielle. Gabrielle, my life has been a colorful road of joy because you are in it.

And to all my siblings: The greatest gift Mom and Dad gave me is you.

CONTENTS

INTRODUCTION	xiii
1. It's A Trap!	1
2. Living In A Fantasy World	8
FAMILY AND GROWING UP	11
3. Steel Reality	13
4. The Ribbons Of My Younger Years	18
5. The Beat Of Confidence In High School	27
QUOTE	39
6. Math Must Submit In College	40
7. Controlling The Grade	47
8. Glass Maker	52
POEM	55
9. The Foundation Of The House: God Is Good	58
10. Enter At Your Own Risk	63
VICTORIES	69
11. Saved By Boxing	71
12. Papers, Papers, Papers	80
13. Success Is The Only Option	84
14. Turncoats	87
15. Approaching The Mountain	96
16. The Walk Of Confidence	103
FAITH	107
17. Friend To Your Soul	109
18. Walking The Red Carpet	113
19. It's A "Lovely Day"	118
20. Holy Excitement	122
21. Holy Surgeon	125
THE DANCE OF LIFE AND COMMERCIAL REAL ESTATE	131
22. You Dance On1 Or On2?	133
23. Pink Is The New Red	142

24. The Fight Will Find You; Put Up Your Dukes	155
25. Matrix In Prada	158
26. We Meet Again	164
27. Own Property	168
Afterword	171
Scriptures	175
Acknowledgments	177
About the Author	181

INTRODUCTION
BOOK COMPASS

It's April 2020, and I hope the current health and economic events do not make the 2008 Great Recession look like a dress rehearsal. I am a Believer, a Believer in Jesus to be exact, and I join a prayer call three times a week. I need it more than ever in my life right now because the world is on lockdown due to the 2020 global pandemic. Business, life, and industry have come to a screeching halt, and I am doing my best to stay mentally and spiritually balanced.

So, I'm sitting in my sunroom typing away on my keyboard in an Atlanta suburb, admiring the company of the newly bloomed dogwood tree nearly kissing my window, allowing nature's sweet perfume to waft through the room. God's creations are unmatched. I first wrote a draft of this book four years ago, but here we are now, in the middle of unprecedented economic and health events. Seems like the country is behaving like a symphony without a conductor, and I sure hope by the time this book is published we will have a sheet of music we can all interpret and execute.

I am a commercial real estate dealmaker and began my career in the shopping center and retail industry. It is the best-kept secret society in America where multimillion-dollar deals are made. I am balancing my time between work and writing this book.

I am a college graduate who has traveled the world and loves business. I thrive on gobbling up knowledge and all that life has to offer. I am a worthy opponent when it comes to negotiating business deals and have been involved in the negotiations of countless seven-to-nine-figure deals and projects over my career. I am also a business muse and love connecting people to new business ideas, business strategy, and profit.

Smile should be my middle name, and I believe an active lifestyle keeps your mind, body, and soul in motion. I stay ready for life's next adventure because sometimes you are on your next adventure within a matter of minutes. Family, friends, faith, and fun are a few of my favorite words that start with an *F*.

Let me tell you what awaits you in the pages of this book so you will have a compass as you read.

I love short stories, so I sectioned this book into four areas that felt natural and engaging: Family and Growing Up, Victories, Faith, and The Dance of Life and Commercial Real Estate.

I wrote this book to tell my dad's story. My dad is an unsung hero. I believe children have the responsibility of carrying on their parents' legacy. His life and parenting will be inspiring to some, so I am introducing him to the world. You will also meet my other hero, my mom.

My goal was to also share how critical both parents are in a child's life. God wanted parents—a mother and father—to raise a child for a reason. I share how important his parenting is to my life as a girl and a woman and how important a father is in raising an African American girl post-civil rights.

I share key life moments and experiences that helped shape who I am and who I am becoming. They happen to contain good advice and insight that can be helpful to many, such as the section on Faith, which I hope will really make you think.

Yes, there's more.

In the section titled Faith, I share my journey from childhood to current day and how I've been called to use the gifts that God has given me, among other topics. You will see scriptures in the book as well. This was a significant decision that took much thought and input from friends. I could not decide if I should put the scriptures as footnotes, put references to the scriptures in the back of the book, or type them out in the body of the text. I chose the latter. I knew most readers would not pay attention to the footnotes or go to the back of the book.

I finished reading the entire Bible two months ago and walked away realizing that it had been hijacked. Many of the sayings we hear, mantras, and information, and positive thinking that is bubbling out of the mouths of public speakers and motivational speakers are, in fact, biblical. Many of the principles and customs that guide our lives are from the Bible, and I wondered why credit is not being given to the source. So, because of this, I included the scriptures in the body of the book.

The Bible has answers to everything and countless situations. There are stories in the Bible where I have gone through a similar situation, read about it in current day, or witnessed some of the same things in the Bible. What was shocking is that the Bible is a page-turner. There is a lot of drama. It is like a soap opera or a reality show. People are just people, and they behave and misbehave just like people do today. I was also elated to walk away daily with words of wisdom and strength. I could feel my spiritual muscles growing.

There are so many beautiful stories in the Bible, and it is an inspiring read. I walked away with an expanded understanding of God. He is so kind and wants to just love on His children all the time, but when He gets angry, look out because he is a warring God. But even then, He may still have grace, mercy, and forgiveness when He hears your plea.

Last, you should know just how powerful the *Word* is. You can speak and use the words in the Bible and move mountains in your life...literally. So, reader, if you have not read the Bible, I would certainly recommend it. It answered a lot of questions for me in all areas of my life and life on this planet. I also learned the terms *logos* and *rhema*. This was a game changer. If you do not know what they mean, stop and go look them up. If you need understanding, contact a pastor or a Bible teacher.

I also talk about racism in the book. First and foremost, I am a child of God and look at people as God looks at us. Racism is a weapon of division from the enemy that uses people who desire wealth or power, who want to inflict pain and manipulation, and people who have the need to feel superior or be idolized. Racism is a sin on many fronts. It is a sin to desire to be idolized and a sin to idolize someone. God has an unlimited amount of abundance that all have access to, so let's go get it together.

My desire is that when you finish reading the last page, you will feel reignited with your purpose, go hug your family, you will never run from a fight for your dignity, you will take dance lessons, invest in commercial real estate, go to college, and laugh daily. I know it's a long list, but you can do it all!

So now that you have a lay of the land, grab your favorite mug and your choice Saturday morning beverage, and I'll meet you on the next page.

May those whose eyes read the words of this book or whose fingers touch its pages be blessed.

Sincerely yours,

Monica

CHAPTER 1
IT'S A TRAP!

THEY TRIED *to kill my daddy!*

It was just a regular day at home in the 1970s, and I was maybe five or six years old.

"What happened to your leg, Daddy?" I asked inquisitively.

Such an innocent question from a child who didn't know bad people existed in the world or that bad things could happen to her family.

My dad didn't hold back. He told me the truth.

He looked me straight in the eye. "One day I went to work, and out of nowhere someone came to me and asked, 'Butch, you want to drive the crane?' I was surprised.

"I was excited and jumped into the seat of the crane, put it into gear, and started moving, and ...*boom*, it blew up. It had been a setup. They rigged it. I was rushed to the hospital, a part of my leg was nearly blown completely off and hanging on by a thread. The white doctor didn't even try to save the entire leg. He cut it off above the knee. They could have saved it!" Dad finished sharing this horrific event, stopped, and looked at me. Me, Monica C. Smith, his young daughter, who was too young to have a care in the world but suddenly faced a conversation adults would have a hard time having.

Dad believed it was an assassination attempt because he regularly spoke out against the unfair treatment of Blacks at his job at the mill in the 1960s. Someone wanted him dead. They amputated his right leg above the knee, and his lifelong nightmare continued.

At twenty-one years old, he involuntarily sacrificed his leg for "the Cause" during one of the most tumultuous times in modern-day America, when the African American civil rights satyagraha was in full swing. He defended himself and refused to be torn from humanity. It was a permanent sacrifice.

This assassination attempt was yet another situation where he narrowly escaped death in the 1960s. He made it through Vietnam in one piece after being drafted into war as a paratrooper in the 101st Airborne Division of the army (also known as Screaming Eagles, the most recognized division of the army), where he was dropped behind enemy lines, only to return home to work at the mill and lose a portion of his leg for standing up for human rights—the right to live and the desire to work at a job that should not endanger your life disproportionately due to your skin tone.

How did he get here, you ask? When he left the army in the early 1960s, he went to work at Globalwest Steel on Second Lake. Everyone worked at one of the mills in Northwest Indiana or the Calumet Region, as it is also called. After a person graduated from high school, that's where they went to work. No degree needed. As economic engines and major job generators in the region, they were good alternatives for Black families and pushed thousands into the middle-income bracket. Mom could stay home and watch the children, and dad would go to work. The salaries were good enough to live a comfortable life.

East Chicago (E.C.), Gary, Hammond, and Whiting, Indiana, were heavy manufacturing cities. The proximity to Lake Michigan, Chicago, rail, air, highways, and top-rated colleges and universities made for an ample and skilled blue-collar and white-collar workforce. Globalwest on Second Lake was a large steel mill with thousands of workers in the 1960s and 1970s.

Many people may not think about how incredibly dangerous it was back then. Today, there is still risk, but manufacturing is more modernized with advances in technology and the creation of organizations such as the Occupational Safety and Health Administration (OSHA), which began in 1970. According to Dad, management gave the most dangerous jobs to Black men. My father continuously complained and pushed management to stop disproportionately endangering them, but it almost cost him his life.

Dad worked in the hottest place on earth—the blast furnace. Imagine walking into the center of a volcano with extra gear on and doing hard labor for hours on end. There is not enough water in the world to quench this thirst and soothe the internal organs from the debilitating heat. The human body was not designed to endure this kind of heat nor those conditions, especially not for days on end. My uncle Kenneth, who also worked at the mill in the 1960s like my dad, tells me they called it BOF for basic oxygen (or oxide) furnace. He said the BOF workers wore face shields and a whole suit that was like a uniform that covered their entire bodies. He said they would check for carbon monoxide but would sometimes get faulty reads. He said it was a dangerous place. He also mentioned that his brother worked at the 24-Inch Bar Mill and would come home with a back brace on due to flipping steel bars.

The blast furnace has not changed much in more than one hundred years. The basic process from the early 1600s is still utilized. Air is blasted into burning concoctions of charcoal, limestone, and iron ore to smelt iron. Working in the blast furnace entailed many dangers in the 1960s, including working in the relentless heat, inhaling toxic fumes, smoke, soot, and deadly gases.

There is still danger today working a mill blast furnace, but thank goodness for the protective gear and carbon monoxide monitors worn by mill workers today. Also, the electric furnace is an alternative to the blast furnace and has increased in popularity. There is also a higher degree of awareness of the health repercussions of exposure to this type of job, and medical treatments have advanced for those who fall ill due to the exposure to the pollutants at the mill. (I'm no expert on blast furnaces, but I did do some research as I prepared this book.)

As long as I can remember, my dad, Verdell Smith Sr., was missing part of his leg. I think back to it, and it just makes me shudder.

Did he see the looks on the culprits' faces when they realized the assassination attempt didn't work—that he was still alive?

He was injured and knew that someone—or some people—around him wanted him dead. He was terrified, and I am sure he looked around for help, and rather than seeing remorse and concern in their eyes, he saw hatred that the attempt to kill him was a failure. I wonder if someone even called the hospital immediately.

I think about pain medication in the sixties and seventies compared to today and how capable it was to mute the pain of losing a portion of a leg. Did the doctors fairly prescribe him the proper medication? How was he after the surgery? How long did it take to recover? What must it have been like to be a world-class boxer who lost a portion of his right leg?

What must it have been like for my mom when she first heard the news and laid eyes on him? How many months and years did it take to console him? Did he cry in front of her at all?

After Dad finished telling me what happened to his leg, I remember I froze. I couldn't digest what he said. I was too young, and I loved him too much to imagine someone would do this to him. I grew up instantly in that moment. I was six going on thirty. I saw the real world for the first time. He looked away because he saw my expressions. I think I just stared at him for a few seconds because it was the most terrible news I had heard in my young life. I was about to cry. I also didn't understand why someone would want to kill my father. It was just too much for my little innocent, pure brain. He quickly left the room once he saw the tears begin to well up in my eyes.

Later, he told me how he loved to work out and train when he boxed. He would run for hours and stare into the sun to absorb its power. But now, he was a machine who had lost its engine.

In the middle of the night, I would awaken to hear his moans and screams of pain. He decided not to take pain medication and was constantly agonized by what likely included phantom leg syndrome. It got really bad some nights. I saw him suffer my entire childhood.

Dad did work at the mill after the incident and during the lawsuit he launched. It had to be tough to go to a job every day with part of a missing limb, looking at the person(s) who tried to kill you. I distinctly remember Mom loading us in the car late at night to pick up Dad from work.

"There he is! There's Daddy!" my younger sister, Gabrielle, and I would yell in unison.

We weren't twins, but sometimes you had to wonder because we did act, think, and talk alike.

I remember the look on his face of love, excitement, and joy to see his family loaded in the car. Thinking back, he stood with such regal charisma and confidence, even when he was waiting for a ride at midnight after a long shift.

Mom asked routinely, "How was work?"

"You already know the answer to that. What's for dinner?" he'd respond, turning the topic to a more pleasing discussion for the fifteen-minute drive home.

"You're going to turn into a buttered lima bean, but I made them again since you mentioned them a few days ago. Everyone has eaten, and I've saved some for tomorrow."

Oh yes, Mom made her family's signature buttered lima beans. These beans were delicious and were practically holy in our house. You needed to have the right amount of seasoning, the right amount of water, and cook them the right amount of time. To this day, this is one of my favorite childhood dishes. Mom would top it off with corn bread and a fried hot dog sliced down the middle. This was five-star eating, my friend. Now I really appreciate all the delicious zinc in those beans.

"How is management treating you?" she pressed, still trying to gauge how things were going. She looked in the rearview mirror several times and studied the oncoming headlights as she spoke to Dad.

"They're keeping their eye on me as usual, but since the lawsuit is getting more serious than they expected, they're changing up their tactics," he responded as he let down the window and turned up the radio, attempting to send a signal to Mom that he didn't want to discuss work.

I remember the long, lonely drive on the edge of Lake Michigan. It was a desolate road used for mill traffic. The lake was massive and had an eerie quiet rhythm at night and some song with "catfish" in the chorus always seemed to be on the radio. I would imagine scary-looking catfish swimming in the opaque black lake and would wish my parents would change the station. We'd head home under the pitch-black sky, whose stars could not wink at me because they hid behind the smoke coming from the mouths of factories. We navigated the maze of highways and roads that twisted and turned as we exited the mill, and once Mom turned onto Cline Avenue, the full moon popped out to follow us back to our safe brick house.

I'd fall asleep on the way home and was awakened by the slow right turn onto our street. Our neighborhood was serene and tranquil. The streetlight shone through the front car window and directly onto my face as I sat in the middle of the back seat, or the "hump seat" as it was nicknamed. Mom gently drove up our steep inclined driveway, and everyone who was asleep in the car was awakened to the slow, lumbering garage door that was steadily lifted by its track. Mom pulled in the garage and everyone exited the car eager to continue their slumber in their own beds.

Dad made a beeline for the kitchen sink, washed his hands, and then swung open the refrigerator door seeking the lima beans. Mom grabbed a plate for Dad.

As I got under the covers, I was comfortable and ready to go to sleep since Daddy was home. I felt safe in my bed, in my quiet neighborhood surrounded by the love of my parents, my siblings, and our pine trees, which stood guard at the perimeter of our home.

CHAPTER 2
LIVING IN A FANTASY WORLD

"Y'ALL LIVING in a fantasy world. This world don't give a fuck about you. You're living in a fantasy world," Dad said intently with a sense of urgency on his face as he paced through the kitchen the next morning.

Oh, that's just Dad again, on his rant, I thought.

I watched him walk through the kitchen like he was about to go scream this phrase from the mountaintop. It was especially common for him to say this after he finished a shift at work. I continued to read my sci-fi book at the kitchen table.

This is the number one phrase I remember from Dad from childhood. The number two phrase was "Always look out for number one." I heard it repeatedly for several years as a young girl through my teenage years. It reverberated through our home and came without warning. You might have been eating a snack in the kitchen, washing dishes, having a conversation, whatever, and out of nowhere came this James Earl Jones–like voice that spewed this phrase as if my siblings' and my life depended on it. Dad said it with anger, as if his children had done something wrong. The phrase and its tone accused us of being out of touch and naïve. It had no hope in its tone and offered no solution.

As I look back, it was really a message of the battles Dad knew his children would need to win. He looked into the future and was angry at what we would face. He painfully understood there was very little he could do but warn us in the most effective way he knew how, and that was with straight-up, uncensored, Black-male-born-in-the-1940s, deep-cutting truths. Sometimes his words, criticisms, and lessons were harsh, militant, direct, blunt, street, and unforgiving. Consequently, they were *all* the things I would need to survive in America as a Black female, especially to succeed in corporate America where money, egos, and "the club" at times ran the show.

It is just amazing to me that his lessons are still relevant decades later. I can tap into this well of endless parameters for life—tips, advice, values, morals, ethics, work tactics, relationships, decision-making, crises, strategies, and more. His advice, life guidance, and teachings were one of the greatest gifts I received as a child.

School had officially begun. My dad's custom-made boot camp to create children who could survive different terrains and circumstances went into session in my early childhood years, and being female by no means gave you a pink pass. This was not ballerina camp, by the way. The sergeant was a Vietnam veteran, championship boxer, and a self-taught genius. Not to mention, a man who lost a portion of his limb at work for simply requesting better work conditions that would not jeopardize his safety. There should have been a warning sign that I would be entering a boot camp when I entered the world because I would have come out boxing.

But Dad did not just get on his soapbox. He had lived and practiced what he taught us with his battles in the courtroom for civil rights, his battles in the boxing ring, and on the battlefield in the Vietnam War. As you read, you will see how he attacked and counterattacked what he encountered in life. He had some gripping and painful experiences, but he stayed in control of his thoughts, and his momentum of thought and body were always moving forward.

I understand why he fought back so hard. When you do not defend yourself or prevent future attacks, you have given permission for the world to deal with you as it sees fit. One becomes a rag doll on an endless roller coaster ride, and this was just not an option for my dad. He awoke every morning prepared to fight for his life and for the lives of his family.

Photo of my Dad

FAMILY AND GROWING UP

In this section, we'll look at select Polaroid pictures of my life growing up in Northwest Indiana. Parenting is a 24/7 job, and being a kid is no cake walk when your parents are on a mission to create productive human beings with purpose and a vigor for greatness. Yet, my parents did it well. Mom and Dad peeked in our bedrooms at night to make sure everything was okay. This simple act alone helps a child feel so much love and protection.

CHAPTER 3
STEEL REALITY

THERE IT WAS. The stark change in the air. Without warning, it just filled your lungs like a sneak attack. It didn't belong there, and your body naturally rejected it, but you needed to breathe to live, so your lungs only took in enough to keep the lights on. The air was filled with the swirling designs of smoke of different hues coming from the bursting smokestacks eager to expunge their cocktail cloud of chemicals.

I was too young to understand what was happening to the environment and the impact it had on the human body. I just remember the factory effluvium that I fought to minimize in my lungs. This dancing smoke was almost hypnotic as it constantly morphed and changed shape from the moment it spewed from the mouth of the stack.

Photo of Steel Mill. Photo credit: Dara's Photography/Super Tigreez Photography

I grew up in East Chicago, Indiana, typically called E.C., in the 1970s and 1980s. Located on the southern edge of Lake Michigan, E.C.'s name stems from the fact it is directly east of the city of Chicago, Illinois.

The following are a few famous people who were born in E.C. [1]

- Kenny Lofton—all-star baseball legend
- Greg Popovich—president and head coach of the NBA's San Antonio Spurs
- John M. Ford—writer, game designer, and poet
- E'Twaun Moore—NBA player

East Chicago was incorporated in 1893 and was the first truly industrial city of Northwest Indiana. According to the city's website, E.C. was known as the most industrialized municipality in the country. It was born of railroad and steel and was originally known as the Twin City. The two sections were called the Harbor and East Chicago. They were separated by an enormous railyard that was a gateway to Chicago and the West. Seventy nationalities lived in E.C., and each brought their churches, culture, and way of life. Declared "Workshop of America" and "Arsenal of America" during World War II, E.C. played an integral part in American history. [2]

Unfortunately, having grown up in E.C., when I moved to New York City in the mid-2000s and got my first smell of air in a neighborhood below 14th Street on the West Side, it stopped me in my tracks. I prayed for clean air in that neighborhood and that city. God led me to purchase an infrared sauna. They are known for extracting heavy metals and pollutants from the cells. I would later find out just how important this waterless portable sauna was for my health treasure chest. New York City firemen used it to detox, and Oprah Winfrey purchased one. After leaving New York City, I went on a heavy metal cleanse and still have a sauna. God always provides a solution.

Okay, where was I?

Back to my home-girl story…

My parents moved to the newer side of town in E.C. with large homes and perfectly manicured lawns. Dad designed the house and had it built in the 1960s. It was a close-knit neighborhood with a mix of hardworking families, doctors, board of education executives, police officers, and stay-at-home moms. Sunday dinners with the family, double Dutch, bell-bottoms, and groovin' music was always playing on the WGCI radio station out of Chicago.

Elementary and middle schools were in walking distance, and the neighborhood was like a village. Gary, Indiana, where Dad had a lot of family, was next door. E.C. was majority Black and Latino with a small percentage Caucasian. It was a small city that had two high schools and later condensed them to one state-of-the-art facility. Since we were near Chicago, we were a part of the Chicago Metro. We grew up watching Chicago TV, rooting for the Bulls, Cubs, Sox, and Bears. My family would also pop over for day trips, and as I got older, my siblings and friends and I would go clubbing in Chicago. I would later move to Chicago. I can proudly say I attended games of the Bulls, Sox, and the Blackhawks. I saw Cubs games via a rooftop in Wrigleyville, a bonus if you have a friend who lives near the stadium.

I was very active in school. I was on the track team, played softball, and joined Top 20, the legendary dance group at my high school. I was vice president of the sophomore class and landed my first job at fifteen at McDonald's. I learned early on I enjoyed public speaking, having won the citywide speech contest during my junior year in high school.

Every summer, my family, including my grandparents on my mother's side, went to the Bud Billiken Parade and Picnic in Chicago. My grandparents packed up their car with an immense amount of delicious food and treats. It was like Thanksgiving in the summer. The Bud Billiken Parade and Picnic is the largest African American parade in the country and began in 1929 in Chicago. Robert Sengstacke Abbott, founder of the *Chicago Defender* newspaper, started the parade. It is held annually in Washington Park and features celebrities, businessmen, politicians, and highlights the youth. Abbott created the Bud Billiken mascot in 1923 to represent the guardian of children. The parade also focuses on education and travels through Bronzeville and Washington Park neighborhoods on the city's South Side.

Mom and my grandmother were exceptional cooks. Everyone had a sweet tooth, so tasty desserts were always on the menu. My grandfather never drove on the highway, so we would take the long, scenic, winding drive from E.C. through Whiting, Indiana. He would head north on Route 41, passing Wolf Lake Memorial Park, then crossing the state border into Chicago and passing through the alphabet avenues located on the Southeast Side. Today, the casinos have commandeered residence in this neighborhood.

For birthdays, Mom baked your favorite cake. I had multiple siblings, and the birthday person was celebrated by everyone singing a birthday song. Red velvet, German chocolate, banana cake, chocolate, and carrot cake were the usual suspects. As a bonus, you got the first and last piece if it was your birthday. Mom eventually started working full-time again, but she still attended every event, made birthday cakes, and home-cooked meals were always ready when we returned from school.

We went to Gary a lot to visit family and hung out at Miller Beach, which had beautiful lake homes and the *phinest* boys in the region. The boys were so good-looking, it would have been a model agency's paradise. Glen Park was another lovely neighborhood in Gary.

Genesis Center in Gary had some of the best events and parties. Lines were around the block to get into their parties, and everyone couldn't wait to get to sweating to hyper house beats and then slow it way down to Keith Sweat. West Side High School was located in Gary and hosted the Jackson 5 for a homecoming concert. My dad would later tell me how Joe, the father of the Jackson 5, worked at the mill and asked him if he should quit his job and fully launch his kids' careers. My dad said he told him to go.

Many students at E.C. schools loved playing basketball with Gary schools. They were so much fun, and their basketball skills were off the charts. During my freshman year, my high school (Washington High School) made it to the state championship. It was a great season.

As I write this, my niece is a track star in Indiana, having won a full scholarship to college. Yes, I am taking a moment to brag about my niece. I am proud of her. She was a straight-A student in high school and is making her name known on her college track team. I guess one could say, it is in the blood, as my uncle and her mother (my sister) were also exceptional in track.

Overall, it was a highly active and safe childhood, but through my entire childhood, I watched Dad fight Globalwest Steel on Second Lake. I call it the modern-day David and Goliath.

---

1. *Retrieved from www.wikipedia.com footnote*
2. *Retrieved from www.eastchicago.com. footnote*

CHAPTER 4
THE RIBBONS OF MY YOUNGER YEARS

AS A LITTLE GIRL in the 1970s, life seemed simple—pretty ribbons, ice cream, swing sets, cartwheels, and the occasional celebrity appearance at a wedding.

"Gabrielle, it's hot out. Let's go play outside," I said as a rush of hot air enveloped my face as I closed the back door.

My younger sister, Gabrielle, walked toward the closet with the dust mop. "Mom said we have to make our bed first and dust mop our room."

"I'll meet you outside."

I burst out the back door of our brick home on a corner lot in Prairie Park, a middle- to upper-income area of E.C. Everyone knew each other, and the neighborhood watched and reprimanded the children… *Ahhh*, the seventies. It was truly a village.

The salmon-colored brick structure always made me feel safe during storms—it was our fortress. As a little girl, it seemed huge and loomed above my fears, keeping its promise to keep me warm and cozy in the winter, and above all, it protected me from any bad things that could be lurking outside at night. I knew if the Big Bad Wolf came along, he couldn't blow our house down. I marveled at our home's size and strength but was also fascinated with the texture of the brick and would gently caress its rough facade. Ever since my childhood, I've loved brick homes.

I headed straight for the swing set in the backyard, which was my utopia for water sports, cartwheels, backbends, riding my Big Wheel, squishing worms, and running from rogue grasshoppers.

Our lot was huge, and the swing set always quenched my thirst for activity. It was sky blue with two swings, a seesaw, and a slide. It also had a dash of silver sprinkles that always glimmered in the sun's reflection, almost like the swing set was winking at me. Sagely pine trees that were there before I was born were distributed throughout our property, standing guard like heavenly soldiers on the perimeter on the northern side of the house and in the front yard. They seemed to always be on watch and gave the home more character, strength, and a regal feel. A line of thick bushes snuggled up against the exterior in the front and back of the house and always made for agonizing weed-pulling weekends. The grass was manicured as were most of the homes in Prairie Park.

"You finished cleaning?" I asked Gabrielle as I went back in the house to check on her progress.

"Yeah…kinda. I swept everything under the bed and in the closet," she said and looked up with a sheepish grin just as our older sister Diane peeked in the room with a smirk of disapproval. She was ridiculously organized and could not stand an unorganized home, dust, dirt, or anything being out of order. Today Diane's home is immaculate, and her organizational skills are likely good enough to run a global company based on her organization in her home, life, and office.

I giggled my approval and said, "Mom will find it. She always looks under the bed. Come on. Let's go down the slide backward before Mom catches us."

"Okay but be careful. Just once, and then we do the seesaw." Gabrielle walked hesitantly.

"Okay, but no jumping off early," I replied.

I was wearing my blue shorts set with a cotton capped sleeve shirt with flowers and matching shorts. Gabrielle wore her favorite tennis girl outfit: white cotton sleeveless Catholic girl shirt with a white mini wrap skirt that tied at the waist. We had our play shoes on from Zayre. We both loved them, so Mom bought a pair for each of us.

We had a large yard, and the grass went to the edge of the street on the north side of our lot—until the city would later seize a portion of our land via condemnation for a sidewalk. Prairie Park was a new development when my parents built. Dad would always complain about the high real estate taxes that came with being on a corner. (Little did I know, I would someday have a career in commercial real estate and work on condemnation cases. It's amazing how much of a sponge you are as a child and the things you remember.)

I absolutely loved our yard, except when I had to pull weeds, which seemed to multiply just from looking at them. The massive pine trees hid secrets that I only knew. There were angels in those pine trees. They would play with me and push me to do higher and faster cartwheels. They always told me they would protect me. If I was sad, I would go outside and the yard, grass, trees, and bushes would all smile and tell me to feel better. If I wasn't in my room indulging in a weekly supply of books from the East Chicago Public Library, I was in our yard. Our yard was my safe place.

The neighbor had a tree that had the sweetest baby apples with a tart aftertaste. Before I ate them, I always prayed they weren't poisonous, but I ate them nonetheless. They were delightful to my young novice taste buds. I took culinary risks, obviously a foodie in the making.

"Hurry up before Rhonda sees us." I'd already eaten five of the baby apples and beckoned Gabrielle to join the smorgasbord before Rhonda, our neighbor and the owner of the apple tree, or Mom caught us.

"They're big this year and so good. Let's take some and hide them in our room for later." Gabrielle stood on her tippy-toes and began grabbing the innocent baby apples, shoving them into her pockets.

"Hide them in your pockets and socks," I urged, "but not too many or Mom will notice."

That night, we ate so many baby apples we fell asleep with them on our pillows and in our hands. Delicious. I had sweet apple dreams.

We had a large patio in the backyard bordered by bushes where Mom grew tomatoes. The next day, Rhonda, who was very quiet, rounded the corner of our home and stepped onto the back patio.

"I have come for payment," Rhonda said as Mom opened the back door and invited Rhonda in. Rhonda had a few tomatoes from Mom's garden in her hand, which she had grabbed on her way to the door.

"Hi, Rhonda. It's so good to see you. Payment for what?" Mom laughed. We didn't see Rhonda much, but when she came over, she had Mom laughing. She had a great sense of humor.

"Payment. You heard me. Payment for all those apples Monica and Gabrielle have been eating off my tree." Rhonda laughed because she was trying to keep a straight face.

"I'm so sorry. I told the girls to stop eating your apples. I'll make sure they stop this time. I can't get Monica to eat vegetables, but she'll eat every apple in sight—in the house and outside the house." Mom shook her head. "I'm glad they like apples, but—"

"Oh, I'm just kidding. I'd like them to be in my daughter's wedding as flower girls. My daughter is in love with them. That's why I'm stopping by. Every time she comes over, she mentions how adorable they are," she said as she grabbed the glass of ice water Mom handed her. "Would you let them be in the wedding? I believe they would have fun." She put her hands in a prayer position.

"Oh, what a touching request. Yes, that would be beautiful, and they would be perfect flower girls. Please send me color details, dates, et cetera. Let's talk about their dresses." Mom guided Rhonda as they walked into our living room, which had the typical plastic-covered furniture of that era, to sit down and get comfortable and catch up on life.

"Come on, come on. We want to be early for the wedding. Where is Gabrielle?" Mom asked as she pulled the curlers out of her hair as she walked into our bedroom. "It seemed like only yesterday that Rhonda asked you girls to be in the wedding, and now the day is here. Time just flew by."

"Gabrielle can't find her ribbons!" I said in an alarming tone.

"What do you mean, she can't find her ribbons? You have ribbons to match the wedding colors, Gabrielle. Gabrielle? Look in the chester drawer"—yes, this is how we said it back then—"in my room, and then come on so I can do your hair."

Mom told us we would be flower girls. Sounded pretty, but we had never been flower girls before, and we were up for the adventure. Gabrielle and I were a year apart, and people always thought we were twins. This was always a shock to us. We wanted to be individuals, but we always got the goo-goo eyes and smiles when people saw us together. So annoying.

Mom grabbed her camera from her closet shelf and set it next to her. "I have to take a lot of pictures. I didn't think you two could get any cuter."

Gabrielle found her ribbons and quickly brought them to Mom as she tried to hold up her dress so she wouldn't trip.

"Come here, Gabrielle. Let me help you put those on." Mom beckoned Gabrielle to come sit on the floor in front of her.

Gabrielle and I wore matching powder blue dresses made by the mother of the bride's seamstress. It was the 1970s, and a lot of women sewed their own wedding dresses back then. They were good quality and fit perfectly. Our dresses had empire waists, were polyester, and hugged the floor. Little white patent leather baby doll shoes peeked from underneath the dresses. White lace ribbon graced our short sleeves and neckline. Long, elegant ribbons were pulled around our waistlines and tied in neat bows in the back. After a mean press and comb* at the hair salon the previous day, our hair was gracefully pulled into ponytails with long, flowing white ribbons.

My pressed hair was straightened using a pressing comb. It was also called a hot comb or straightening comb. Then my hair was curled with a marcel curling iron. Both were heated in a small custom-designed oven/stove. Sometimes the comb was placed on the open flame of gas stoves. I had a lot of hair, and that comb was smoking hot...literally! Needless to say, I did not like going to the beauty salon growing up!

Flower Girl

We arrived at the church before our scheduled time. I got a glimpse of the bride as we grabbed our baskets with rose petals, which were sitting on a sofa behind the bride. I remember thinking how the bride stared in the mirror with such a look of peace on her face. Reader, isn't true love peace? I was more nervous than she, and I was only dropping petals on the ground. She turned around and came over to Gabrielle and me and thanked us for being her flower girls. After she gushed over our cuteness, she gave us a hug and a kiss on our foreheads and sent us on our way to head down the aisle.

I was petite with seventy percent eyes and thirty percent smile. My teachers called me moon and saucer eyes and always gave me a big smile when they saw me.

The wedding guests kept twisting in their seats looking toward the back of the church awaiting our entrance. The flower girl music from the wedding dress rehearsal was being played by the organist. That was our cue. Time for the show to start, and I was super nervous. I wished the flower petals would jump out the basket and lay themselves on the floor. I was not ready for all this attention—unless I was dancing of course.

Rhonda went up to my mom with the biggest smile I had ever seen. The wedding was over, and the bride and groom floated out of the church on a cloud of love. Rhonda thanked Mom for letting us be flower girls. Our flower girl performance was a success. We headed toward the front exit of the church, through the double glass, tinted doors, and down the concrete stairs where the bride and groom took some of the most important photos of their young lives. We slowly walked toward our car as we soaked up the last moments of the occasion.

"Monica, why did you walk so fast?" Mom asked as she patted me on the shoulder. "You did a great job though."

"I was nervous. All those people were staring at me."

"I looovveed it. I could do it again and again and again." Gabrielle skipped down the sidewalk in front of us toward the car door. Mom loaded us into the car for the ride back home.

The wedding was at our church, which was on the other side of E.C. It was a traditional Baptist church that could have been in the Deep

South or in the north because of the architecture, décor, and the spirit-filled walls. You could feel the centuries of perfection in the gospel songs and notes. This is the music we created to soothe our souls, wounds, and atrocities against our people. This self-medication continued through the generations, showing its head in other music genres created by African Americans such as jazz and early rap.

Those four walls with stained-glass eyes also saw weddings, baptisms, graduation honors, spirits blessed as they made the journey back home to the Lord thy God, and numerous accomplishments celebrated. It was the meeting place for our people, and it taught you how to wear a "mean" hat...with style, grace, sophistication, and a touch of attitude.

By the time I came of age, the classy-lady-in-a-hat era had simmered, but it was alive and well through my younger years.

We looked lovely in our dresses, and our brown skin had already been touched by the summer sun. My skin was a beautiful caramel color, and Gabrielle's was a rich lovely toffee complexion. We carefully got into the car and made sure our dresses were fully in the car as well.

"You two deserve a treat." Mom put the car in gear.

"Dairy Queen. Yeah, Mommie, yeah. We do deserve a treat," Gabrielle said with glee as she jumped up and down in her seat, totally forgetting she had on a long dress.

"Ice cream sandwich for me," I chimed in as I looked to Mom for acknowledgment of my request. "What will you get, Gabrielle?"

"A sundae since Sunday is tomorrow, and no nuts, Mom, remember?" Gabrielle said.

"Yes, I remember. Nuts make your mouth feel funny," Mom said as she nodded.

"What will you get, Mom? You deserve a treat too," I said as I turned left in the front passenger seat and looked at Mom while she drove.

"You pick for me, Monica. What should I get?" Mom asked.

"You eat the Dilly Bars so fast, so I say get a Dilly Bar," I said.

"Excellent choice," Mom said as she turned the corner onto Columbus Drive, one of the main streets in town. The famous Zel's Roast Beef was on the same street and had the best roast beef and chili hot dogs in E.C.

Dairy Queen was on our way home, and she turned right into the parking lot. Our taste buds started to dance at the sight of the red-and-white logo.

"Don't slam the door shut, but make sure it's closed, and lock the doors. Gabrielle, keep your flower basket in the car. It'll be here when you get back. Hold up your dresses, you two. You look so beautiful today, and you did a wonderful job as flower girls. I can't wait to see the pictures." Mom shuffled in her white patent leather purse for her wallet as all three of us walked toward the call of ice cream.

CHAPTER 5
THE BEAT OF CONFIDENCE IN HIGH SCHOOL

"I HAVE to be on the ready at all times. I wonder what the flow will be today," I said to myself as I walked into E.C. Washington High School's gymnasium in the mid-1980s.

It was packed to the rafters. I glanced up at the fifteen-foot replica of my uncle, Dale Johnson, hanging from the ceiling. He won a state championship in track in 1971, and the school continued to honor his achievement. It was so cool to know he walked the same grounds to practice track and basketball. Washington High was built in 1898. Generations of students attended this school, and now it was my turn. I was a freshman who was about to lay a funky-fresh performance on the pep rally.

"You ready?" the school's rapping super star Reggie Brooks asked as he looked ahead with the killer instinct he had every time we were about to perform. He smiled, took a glance at his Swatch watch, and waited for me to respond as the crowd started a low roar.

Anticipation was the adrenaline the crowd and the performers fed on. I loved it. It was irreplaceable. The moment before a performance was a suspended moment in time dripping with excitement.

"You know this," I quickly replied as I flashed a smile that let him know we were about to take this crowd to the mountaintop of hip-hop.

Reggie laughed and shook his head because this was something he always said, so it was my way of letting him know we were about to kill it Awesome One style. Awesome One was Reggie's rapper name.

He walked in first, and the people in the crowd lost their minds. They knew what was coming. They were about to feast on the performance of a mastermind artist who just happened to be their schoolmate.

I scanned the audience and saw a sea of maroon and white, our school colors. People were jumping to their feet as soon as he walked in.

"Now, what you all have been waiting for: another incredible performance by Reggie Brooks plus Monica Smith," the announcer screamed into the mic as the crowd roar hit higher decibels.

I confidently walked in behind him, getting my instrument ready for action, and the chanting began.

"Awesome One…Awesome One…Awesome One," the crowd said in unison while they stood up, then sat down in a synchronization doing the wave, which was them giving a form of respect to the performer. Some called it the ripple, and it was commonly seen at sporting events.

Reggie was the best rapper in East Chicago. He only rapped impromptu, off the cuff—you know, the original way rap was born.

---

beatboxing

[beet-bok-sing]

A musical style or technique, especially in hip-hop, in which the sounds and rhythms of percussion instruments or a drum machine are simulated by using the mouth and voice.[1]

I walked in ready to pounce on the beat. I had on jeans, freshly pressed hair, and a red short-sleeve T-shirt. I was comfortable. People knew

Reggie, but this was our first big performance on a grand stage in front of our classmates. Up until then, I had been slaying unsuspecting victims (boys) in the hallways and schoolyard. The pressure was on.

As I walked in, the people who knew my talents started clapping faster and threw their fists in the air. Everyone else just looked inquisitive, not sure why I was there.

Reggie stepped to the mic, and as soon as he opened his mouth, the crowd roared again. He waited about thirty seconds for them to sit down again.

He yelled, "Hey, everyone! Thanks for the applause! It means a lot!" He smiled and straightened out his Ralph Lauren light green button-down shirt, which was hanging beneath his Ralph Lauren ocean blue sweater. His preppy top met his cool rolled-up jeans and dark blue moccasins.

The crowd had finally simmered down, and he said with the excitement of a sports announcer, "You know I'm bringing the rhymes for you today, but before we begin, I want to introduce you to Monica Smith, aka Lady Box. Please help me welcome her. She'll be dropping the soundtrack for my *skillz* today." He turned to look at me as he emphasized the word *skillz*.

The crowd cheered—or at least some of them. Those who knew me knew their ears were about to get schooled.

"A one two, one two," Reggie spit out rhythmically and quickly as a warning to the crowd to listen up and a signal for me to feel where he was flowing that moment in vibe, tone, emotion, and speed.

I was a little nervous, but a good nervous. I internalized the nerves and recycled the energy into strength, stamina, and clarity and used it to elevate above the situation. No fear, as my daddy taught me.

I tuned my antennae to the creative rhythms circulating in the hip-hop atmosphere where all the great artists of the day went for artistic food. Hip-hop was an ever-changing machine of creativity so you kept your creative mind open to receive and be inspired moment by moment. I stepped on the gas, and my first note was a smooth, elastic deep bass that got louder and deeper as I held the note. A girl loved bass, so that's usually how I started out to let the crowd know I was not *playin'*, and I could drop a beat. They needed to know who was on the mic, and I was the real deal. The sooner the shock wore off that I was a petite—five foot two—girl, the sooner they could enjoy the performance and take this beatbox ride.

Let's see if I can get them to stand up for a lady, I said to myself.

My first bass note was so deep you wouldn't think a girl could do it.

Several people in the crowd immediately stood to their feet.

That's right, stand up for the lady, I said to myself.

"You have got to be kidding me," a jock on the front row mouthed. He was sitting about five feet from me. He instinctively put his hand to his mouth in shock, then turned to his left and looked at his teammate sitting next to him.

They both just stared at each other, then looked back at me and started to shake their heads to my beat. After they got over the initial surprise of the five instruments that came out of my mouth at the same time, the crowd started to sway to my interpretation of beatboxing. I had my own style, and it was contagious.

Reggie was in stealth mode. You didn't see where he was going, but he got there fast and got the job done. He bobbed and weaved, using his words as rhythmic, hypnotic invitations to take a hip-hop journey like no other. As his beatboxer, I was just in awe. He managed to rap on any topic at any time at the drop of a hat. He rapped in the moment, and you heard different verses every time he rhymed.

A modern-day poet.

At this point, I stopped looking at the crowd. I focused on anticipating Reggie's flow. He kept changing and rearranging the rhythm, so I had to be practically telepathic to stay in sync. I was one hundred percent living in the notes in that moment and did not care who was looking at me and what they were thinking. Sometimes, I took the wheel and led the flow or rhythm of the rap. I think my love for dance helped me be a good beatboxer. I rarely listened to words in a song. I solely focused on the beat and how it made me feel and move. Because of this, I had an innate musicality. Not to mention, I'd been studying violin since elementary school.

Reggie ended the performance by fast-forwarding his speed. It was punchy and potent. It was almost as if he beatboxed while he rapped. When he rapped, you felt like he looked you straight in the eye, not blinking. That's how direct and intentional his words were. His pauses and voice levels were masterfully placed like he was in the studio cutting a record. After he finished the roller coaster of his last verse, the crowd jumped to their feet again.

They chanted "Awesome One" again.

Reggie thanked the crowd. "What did you think of Lady Box?" he yelled as he turned to his right to look at me as he clapped a few times as approval.

The crowd screamed and started chanting my name and his. I was still in the beatbox zone, so my body was still vibrating from the beats. I came back to earth, smiled, and we walked out, turning around to wave at the crowd one more time.

We had no idea we were in the belly of the hip-hop institution. Rap and hip-hop were in their infancy, so you just went with it and put your stamp on your style—pure fun, let me tell you. The artistry created during the mid-eighties set the tone and the standard for this new genre, which took not just the community but the world by storm.

So, what may seem like just having fun had a foundation in courage and gave me the audacity to believe I could do something outside of the norm. Not only did I have to believe I could have the skill of beatboxing, I also had to have the moxie to perform it and not once did I think I couldn't do it.

"That was amazing," I said, excited as we exited the gymnasium and headed straight for the water fountain down the hall.

"The crowd… Did you hear that? You would have thought we had just won the homecoming game," Reggie said as he followed me. "We got a standing ovation."

I was beaming. "I can't believe it. This is so much fun." I took a few gulps of water from the fountain, twirled around, then gave him a serious look. "You really should think about a professional career. I know you mentioned you have to go to college. Can't you do both?"

"My mom isn't having it," he responded quickly as if he instinctively knew the question was coming.

"Okay, okay, I get it." I nodded because I knew my parents were very strict with college.

"Reggie…Monica," the tenth-grade English teacher yelled as she ran out of the pep rally.

We turned around to see Ms. Blake running toward us. She asked if we would perform at an elementary school on the other side of town. We accepted the invitation on the spot and agreed to speak to her the following day during lunch.

Wow. We had our next gig.

As we spoke to Ms. Blake, several classmates came out and surrounded us, begging us to do an encore. Never one to disappoint, I started hip-hop dancing first, did a quick turn, and as I turned around, shot off a machine-gun base beat with fancy footwork to match. One of the classmates was so shocked he fell out on the floor, which was a sign of his approval. Reggie came in with a tongue-twister rhyme that kept tempo with my machine-gun rhythm. I danced and beatboxed at the same time, and by then, we were surrounded by over fifty people, including teachers. Reggie caught my dancing groove and matched my dance moves without breaking a sweat while he rapped. The performance was so good, someone put down their hat and people began dropping money in it. I'm telling you, the best things in life happen suddenly, when you least expect them.

Reggie and I had a blast that day. We ended the second performance, grabbed the money, bowed to the crowd, and headed to our next class. The entire school had taken a break for the pep rally, but now it was time to get back to the books. Science, one of my favorite subjects, was my next class. I grabbed my science book out of my locker and walked in the door with a minute to spare before the bell rang.

"Yeah, I remember that day. That show was dope..." Reggie's voice trailed off as we reminisced in 2021 about our performances back in da day—the 1980s.

He mentioned that a door opened for a potential record deal after high school, but he went to college and sailed off to a successful career and a happy marriage with children. He reached out to me on Facebook to share a video of his son, who is rapping and following in his footsteps.

"I can't believe you have this," he whispered in shock after I texted him a picture of the cassette tape with him performing a rap dedication to me, aka Lady Box, back in the 1980s.

"I know. I just found it. I was looking for something else and came across these tapes. I knew I had some 1980s beatboxing tapes but was beyond elated to see your name on one of them. It actually says *Reggie Raps to me and*—"

"Did you listen to it?" he asked with excited anticipation.

"No. I need to get them digitized. These tapes are so old I'm taking them to a company tomorrow to be transferred. I found a pretty reputable company in Atlanta that can do it." I stared at the tape in disbelief. "If you hear it on iTunes in a few weeks, it wasn't me. I could make money on them," I joked.

We shared a few more memories and ended the conversation. He was on break and needed to get back to work, and I was typing away on my manuscript attempting to make my publishing deadline.

Reggie and I performed countless times together in high school. I also performed with other male and female rappers. It was a blast. I appreciated my family's support and one of my buddies Eric, who came to many of my shows from Gary Weesstiiide.

A few weeks later, I pulled up to the discreet one-story tan building where the cassette tape digitization company was located.

"There is no way God would preserve these tapes for decades for there not to be anything on them," I said to myself while I said a little prayer the tape would be in good condition. I pulled into a parking space, smiled, created a positive outcome in my mind, grabbed hold of hope, and thanked God for keeping safe this keepsake.

"How can I help you?" said the guy behind the desk as I walked up to the pickup counter.

"Monica Smith. I have a cassette order," I said with a pleading look.

He handed me the order.

"Is there anything on it?" I immediately asked while I stared at him without blinking.

"Yes. We wouldn't charge you if there was nothing on it," he said with confidence to reassure me I'd gotten my money's worth.

As I curiously asked him about the major commercial real estate development under construction outside his door, I whipped out my credit card, grabbed the small, clear bag with a CD and a zip drive enclosed, and turned to leave.

I didn't waste time. I pushed the CD into my car CD player, pushed play, and immediately entered a portal back in time. Reggie and his deejay friend dedicated an entire set to me. The beats were cold, the mix was money, the rapping was solid, and the musicality was dope. Familiar food for the hip-hop soul.

I would pay for this today.

I slowly drove home as I submerged myself in the old-school hip-hop blasting from my Bose car speakers. The music had survived! Good music will never die! It was 2021, and the digitization worked. Once I arrived home, I dashed in my house and inserted the zip drive in my laptop and saved the digitization of the tape.

I emailed and texted Reggie a copy and awaited his response. I wondered how he'd feel hearing himself rap decades later. I put the tape, CD, and zip drive in a safe place and looked at the remaining tapes that needed to get digitized. I couldn't wait to hear what was on them. I didn't remember Reggie and his deejay friend dedicating a performance to me, but I was glad I still had it after all these years. I'll cherish this tape for years to come.

So how did my beatbox journey start, you ask? Good question, and I have answers:

- *You can do anything.*
- *Fear nothing.* (Dad despised fear.)
- *Say no to doubtful or weak thinking…*which pretty much sums up my upbringing.

These statements at a very young age translated into *be bold, take risks, be the first, go for it*. So yes, because of my upbringing, I didn't tell myself I couldn't beatbox because I was a girl, I didn't know how to rap, et cetera. I just looked in the mirror one day and wanted to do it. I opened my mouth, and it poured out perfectly in tone, rhythmic with creativity. It shocked me at first, so I ran upstairs like nothing happened and went down to the basement the next day, looked in the mirror, tried it again, and it happened again… Before I knew it, I was jammin' to The Fat Boys' signature beats on my first try. (I also listened to beatbox royalty Doug E. Fresh and Biz Markie. I created a beatbox tribute to Biz in 2021. May he rest in peace.)

After I finished my first one-person concert in the mirror, I knew I had to tell Gabrielle. She could keep my secret until I fully grasped this new talent of mine. I ran upstairs and found her washing dishes on what was probably the most beautiful summer day ever.

"Hey. I have something to tell you," I said to Gabrielle as I exited the basement and entered the kitchen.

"What's wrong with you?" She spun around while her hands were dripping wet with water and suds. Lucky for her, it was her month to do dishes.

I quietly stepped into the kitchen, looked around to see who was in there, and repeated, "I have something to tell you, I think." I looked around again, just to make sure no one else was entering.

Gabrielle and I were like two peas in a pod, and I could tell her anything.

"You look shocked. What's going on?" she said, clearly looking annoyed that it was seventy-five degrees outside on a Saturday, and she was scrubbing dishes.

"I–I think I can beatbox," I robotically said.

Gabrielle started to laugh and turned back to do the dishes. "What? Let me hear it."

I start out with a basic base beat, then moved ever so eloquently into a Fat Boys rendition.

Gabrielle turned completely around, and with the suds and water dripping on the floor, she said under her breath, "Wait until they hear this at school."

So that was how my beatbox journey started. Confidence, curiosity, crushing the norms/rules...a good formula that I continue to live by today. I was fifteen-ish, and not once did I contemplate the fact that I was a girl and that beatbox was a male-dominated talent pool.

That's because Dad didn't raise genders.

He curated conquerors.

As you will see in the next chapter, it's this confidence, as well as prayer, that finally helped me have a standoff with math. It's no surprise I ended up in a male-dominated industry like commercial real estate.

Thanks for the memories, Lady Box. *Microphone drop.*

But, hold up, wait a minute. Is she back? In 2016, I began jazz scatting and beatboxing at the same time. Stay tuned.

What follows is my 2021 rap dedication to the Awesome One. I have a few rapping *skillz* myself. It was fun times had by all. Peace out.

I have to make sure I am staying ahead of his momentum

My beats gotta be intuitive

Because this lyrical poet is always changing, rearranging, his lines

And I must keep time

So that his sublime rhymes have a beat that will perpetuate his soul's vibration

And translate the meaning to the hip-hop nation

It's a telepathic connection, you see

No way, no how, you can be this fly, unrehearsed, impromptu

Without warning, we are rhyming and flowing, moving and grooving

Jamming the jam session during the high school lunch session

In the courtyard

Where the best urban scholars come to brawl

This urban wordsmith is an expressive genius

And I must match him word for word, flow for flow

Or that is the end of our show

---

1. *www.dictionary.com*

"You are living in the misery caused by the absence of your words."

Bishop Matthew L. Brown, Greater Community Church of God in Christ, Marietta, Georgia
Sermon: July 17, 2022—11 AM Service

CHAPTER 6
MATH MUST SUBMIT IN COLLEGE

"FEAR NOTHING."

Gabrielle and I were sitting in the kitchen, and Dad leaned down to look me in the eye. This was the umpteenth time he'd said it, so I just respectfully stared back.

"Repeat after me: Fear is the enemy. You can do anything you set your mind to," he continued. "We were kings and queens!"

He looked at me for a second to see if what he said registered. I was eight years old and had grown accustomed to the barrage of conscious and subconscious messaging Dad would throw my way. Sometimes he would just be passing through a room and say it. Once he saw and heard my verbal acceptance, he pushed back from the table, grabbed his plate, and headed back to the pot of simmering beef stew for seconds.

Every word Dad said was very intentional when it came to raising me and my siblings and preparing us. This started at a very young age. As I look back, I wonder if a lot of parents started giving their children the harsher side of reality as young as Dad did us. I'm sure he was more intense because he was raising children who were Black.

There was no grace period. The quicker he could infuse the realities of the world, as well as a conquer-all mindset in our thought process, the quicker it would become an innate part of us. He really understood the power of influence a father had on his children. He really understood the delicate mind of a child and the unrelenting and unforgiving world that awaited. He understood that life and situations come fast and that your actions dictate outcomes and have a lasting impact. He respected his role as a father and knew the time he and Mom had to groom and raise us was precious and fleeting.

Many times, there was a desperation in his voice and a look on his face as if he was begging my brain to understand. He repeated the teachings and studied my face and body language anxiously and intently and waited for the moment it would connect to my intelligent awareness. And when he saw it—the lightbulb light up—he exhaled without even realizing it. There was a moment of celebration in his face because he knew he had landed the dismount. His words were surgically precise, his timing impeccable. He caught me off guard when my mind was open so I received the message.

I think today, people really understand that children are very, very impressionable at a young age, but Dad knew this early on and was before his time. He always spoke to me like I was an adult. He did not dumb down his conversation one bit. He propelled my thinking so that I could understand him with an adult mind. He pulled my thinking up, rather than waiting for it to catch up. He knew he could wire a child's mind, and he set out to do so. Before I knew that there should be a message, he was giving me a message. As soon as I could form words and thoughts, he began planting the seeds of success and survival. He wanted survival, success, intelligence, and boldness to be part of my DNA. He wanted these traits to be my default and not an afterthought. He wanted it to be instinct and part of my involuntary response. He wanted it to be in the facts section of my brain. He wanted it to be part of my common sense so that nothing false made sense.

I remember one of his famous sayings was "That is nonsense." I first heard the terms *deductive* and *inductive reasoning* from Dad as a child.

My father inhaled knowledge and read books of multiple topics. We had a line of bookshelves in the basement with topics from psychology to astronomy.

Dad would pull random books and say, "Here. Read this." Then he studied your response as you took the book and read the title. And of course, you could never ask what a word meant. You had to go pull the dictionary and find out for yourself. Oh, how annoying that was.

So, the well of confidence I drew from to beatbox was the same well of confidence I had to return to lasso math under control.

———

It was my first year of college in the late 1980s, and calculus was taking no prisoners. I'd received my grade from a recent test and walked out of class wondering how to fix my math performance. I was an excited student who loved knowledge. I sat at the front of the class and gobbled up every word the teacher said. I respected teachers and their role. I took meticulous notes and was optimistic that I would earn a good grade.

Then came Mr. Math. I disregarded the advice given to take a placement test before college. This was a *big* mistake. I urge all college students to take the math and English placement tests. Had I done this, I wouldn't have had the following experience, but perhaps it was needed to teach me the power of prayer and the power of your thoughts and intentions. I should also mention that I could not always see the board (I should have told my mom) in elementary and middle school, which resulted in angry math teachers and not the best grades in math. The teachers were not aware I could not see the board so they could not understand why I was not picking up faster in class.

I just should have taken the placement test! The leap from high school to college math can be a large one, depending on where you started in college and left off in high school. For me, the summer before college, I seemed to float on a cloud of happiness, feeling freedom for the first time since kindergarten, so the last thing I felt like doing was taking a placement test.

All parents and teachers, regardless of the child's interest, should spend an extra amount of time instilling joy, comfort, understanding, and confidence toward math and science so children know the basics of these subjects. If they are majoring in music, still make sure they understand the basics of math. Colleges are now more heavily exposing their liberal arts majors to math and science courses. Science and English were my favorite subjects in school, but I learned to enjoy math once I learned its rules.

The following scripture is an example of one that is the perfect fit for this chapter. The fear of math is the mountain. We all encounter mountains in our lives. It's what you do with the mountain that matters. I read the scripture out loud and insert the fear. The Bible is overflowing with affirmations, positive sayings, and fighting prayers. They are powerful, and I use them regularly.

For verily I say unto you, that whosoever shall say unto this mountain, "Be thou removed, and be thou cast into the sea," and shall not doubt in his heart, but shall believe that those things which he saith shall come to pass, he shall have whatsoever he saith (Mark 11:23 KJV).

Back to my math story. After the most recent grade on my college math test, I thought about the teachings of Jesus to not fear. I also thought about the words of my dad regarding fear. He spoke about fear like he was kicking it out of existence.

I remember my dad looked at me sternly, saying, "Fear nothing," so I got mad because I knew I had the power to conquer fear. When I saw the 2019 Harriet Tubman movie, I noted the fact that the minister told Harriet to "fear nothing" before she made her first of many escapes. That was the best direction he could have given her.

Here is another scripture I speak out loud regularly when it comes to fear.

> *For God hath not given us the spirit of fear; but of power, and of love, and of a sound mind* (2 Timothy 1:7, KJV).

It starts in the mind, so we must conquer it in the mind. Many books are written with affirmations and positive sayings. What many people do not realize is that many of the sayings stem from the Bible. There are too many to count, but they are there for us. I turn to the Word for inspiration and power and share scriptures throughout the book.

Math is a universal language. What I learned to love about it is it's absolute. After living in a world full of subjective thoughts, opinions, and viewpoints, math became a breath of fresh air—a relief that once I understood its rules, its demands, and its language, I could conquer it and get in sync with its logic and would be welcomed in its world.

I got on my knees and prayed with vigor, faith, and trust that my affirmative prayers would be answered. I was around nineteen years old at the time. Thinking back, my affirmations were along these lines:

I will conquer math, in the name of Jesus. I do not fear math. I get good grades in math. I am excited about math. I will get As and Bs on my math tests, and I will study and understand what I study. I will retain what I study.

I declared victory with a boldness that God gives us because He told us He is listening and to just ask.

I knew to continue college, I had to succeed in math. I excitedly went down one math level and walked away with a B. After that, I changed my major from communications to business management and had to take business calculus. I saw the look on my teacher's face when my grades changed. From that point forward, I got Bs in every math class.

Math is the friend that always gives it to you straight. There is only one right answer all the time every day in any language, galaxy, and country. I was amazed how math really runs the world and continued to need it in several classes. I learned to love math problems like candy and enjoyed the challenge and opportunity to prove to myself that all is possible.

It was a Monday afternoon, and my college math teacher had spent all weekend grading papers. I felt humbly confident about my performance.

"A B-plus!" the teacher just blurted out loud, not realizing the words had just spilled out of his mouth.

"Oh, thank God," I said, and looked up at him beaming like I was accepting an award.

He was taken aback by his involuntary speaking. A look of apology came across his face because of the tone of his voice.

I smiled, looked at the paper, and looked back at him.

A sister—she was a Believer—sitting next to me chimed in, "Amen to that" as the teacher continued passing out test results.

I saw him look over at me a few times with a perplexed expression.

Now that I had had a conversation with math, it said, "I am not your enemy. I am on your side. Respect me and what I can do for you. Welcome to your future, and may I bid you an early congrats on your college graduation."

So, math and I gained a mutual respect. We saw eye-to-eye and rode off into the sunset with calculators, sharpened pencils, and extra erasers in tow.

"Have a great week, everyone," I said as I left class and glanced back at my teacher, who was in shock. I walked out of class feeling lighter, brighter, and the rise in my grade point average.

As I headed to my car in the college campus parking lot, I thought back to the educational standoff I had with Dad in my childhood. It was a game changer, a moment that reestablished the trajectory of my educational future. I'll share it in the next chapter.

PS: Math always gets the last word, so it said as I left class: "Go ye forth and calculate, compound, and solve."

Is not my word like as a fire? saith the Lord; *and like a hammer that breaketh the rock in pieces?* (Jeremiah 23:29 KJV)

CHAPTER 7
CONTROLLING THE GRADE

I BELIEVE I was in middle school at the time, and Mom hand delivered my recent report card to Dad like she'd done ever since I'd started school. This was a little ritual they had for my siblings and me. If you didn't receive feedback, that meant you made it to live another school season.

Dad looked at me with a mixture of unbelief and realization. Next thing I knew, I was being dragged through my home by my hair. My mom, who stood by during the conversation on high alert, screamed as soon as Dad reached for my hair. Tears flew from my eyes as Dad proceeded to pull. This lasted what seemed like hours. I honestly don't know what he said while it was happening, but I would imagine it was "You are going to get good grades. You are going to…"

I knew school and good grades were a top requirement in the house, but for some reason, I became lax. I had a bad report card with some grades that were below a C and grades that had something in common with the word David, and then had the audacity to have a bad semester, which showed I was not putting in much effort toward my education. This was an A-or-B-preferred household, so this was not good. When Mom took him the really bad report card, things got serious quick, fast, and in a hurry.

Dad yelled, "Monica, come here!"

I knew that tone, and I knew this wasn't going to bode well for me. When Dad called a personal face-to-face meeting, I started to pray. Therefore, it's good to get kids in church early so they can pray to Jesus for help when they've been unruly, and God can save them from their parents—or at least play the referee and be the voice of reason. The Word does say spare the rod and spoil the child, so Jesus may be like, *Yeah, you deserve this reproof.*

Dad tilted his head to the side, planted both feet firmly on the ground, and asked, "What is this? Look at these grades." He was clearly getting in discipline parent posture.

I looked at him with a "whatever, dude" look and commented as such. I was living my best childhood life, and it was apparent I had little concern with the recent grades and what poor grades could do to my educational future.

So this was the brief conversation that led to this extreme disciplinary action.

My life passed before me as I was dragged through the house by my long beautiful, freshly pressed hair that cascaded down to my mid-back.

My mom ran behind Dad the entire time screaming, "Let her go! Stop! Verdell, you are going too far! She's a child!" He kept going, and I kept crying.

I did get a quick peek at his face. I had to. I had to gauge just how mad he was so I could determine when this bad dream was going to end. I'm sure there was some pleading in between my tears, but I'm too proud to admit it. Yup, Dad's daughter.

As I looked back, there wasn't anger on his face. Maybe he didn't appreciate that he was disrespected. I would say there was also awareness, and his actions really reflected fear because he knew I was at a crossroads. It tore him apart to hurt me like that, but he felt he had to get my attention. I just didn't give a darn, and that's what shocked and scared him the most. He felt he had to put the fear of God in me because if my grades didn't improve—and improve quickly—I wouldn't get in college, and that of course wasn't an option.

Thankfully, this was the only time he exerted this type of discipline. I wouldn't be where I am today if Dad hadn't stepped in and rescued my educational future. Mom and I picked up the few pieces of my hair that had come loose from around the house, my sore roots healed, and Dad and I never had to have that conversation again. I turned my grades around in middle school and kept striving for good grades because I knew I was destined for college.

I have vivid memories of being told I was going to college for as long as I could comprehend the English language. It was a constant message my dad blurted out every opportunity he could. I could be coming in the house from playing in the yard, and he would just blurt it out. At the time, it was quite annoying, but it worked. I began at a young age putting the pieces together and deciding what I wanted to do with my life. My mom was also a college activist in my life, and the two of them put on the full-court college pressure throughout my childhood.

Young Monica

Years later while in college…

It was the moment I'd been waiting for. Drumroll, please: bringing home an excellent report card from college. I had absolutely no idea there would be so much math when I majored in business management, marketing. Because I attended an engineering school (Purdue University), additional math was on the menu in some form or fashion every semester it seemed…great.

Once I had tamed the math beast, I hit the dean's list jackpot several times. The first time I handed my report card to my mother, I listened attentively, not even breathing or blinking as she took it into her and my father's bedroom. I heard some whispers, but I knew what he was thinking: *She did it. I knew she could do it.*

All those years Dad and Mom spent pushing me toward college worked.

I so badly wanted to say, "In yo' face...nah." But I dared not. He never said anything, which was typical. No news was good news.

He would have said, "Why is this not straight As?" No compliment meant he wanted me to keep reaching for my best. His expectations for his children were without limit.

College Graduation Picture with Mom

CHAPTER 8
GLASS MAKER

"IT WAS A LONG DAY, and I am so glad to get in bed," Mom said as she took a sip of the glass of water next to her bed. Her rollers were rolled tight and right like a can of sardines. She put on her purple scarf, set her mental alarm in her head, and let the mattress brace her fall.

It was 8:30 p.m., and Mom lay down in her and my father's queen bed. As long as I can remember, Mom fell asleep early. One minute you would see her, and the next minute she would be gone, out for the count until the wee hours of the morning. She was dedicated to that routine, but she was up early cooking and cleaning even before the rest of the family woke up. The only evidence of her early waking was food in the Crockpot or a pot of food on the stove and the smell of cleaning products swirling through the house.

My parents had the main bedroom, and it was where we watched TV throughout the day as a family. We sat on their bed or on the floor with our backs leaned up against the bed. We had four TVs in the house, and their room was the cozy place to watch TV.

"Monica," Dad said in the *hey, you better listen up* tone.

I stood as if I was guarding the TV for dear life. Staring, not blinking, at the screen. I watched in awe and appreciation as the bionic man (on

The Six Million Dollar Man series) supposedly ran with superhuman speed. He had a gladiator look as he pursued the villain who had the superhero's damsel in distress in the back seat of a car.

Wow, I thought. *I wish I could run that fast.*

"Monica," Dad said with a mild sense of urgency.

I thought I heard him, but I was very focused on the TV. Now the hero jumped onto the roof of a building as he pursued using his superhuman strength. He didn't even need a cape. I hadn't missed one show yet that year. If I had to choose between watching it and eating grape Now and Laters, the show would've won. The superhero was handsome and was a welcome image to my young eyes. I was around seven years old, so too young to date, but I knew a good-looking man when I saw one.

This was when TV shows were highly monitored and the entire family watched. Fast-forward to today and it's a free-for-all. I grew up with pure and wholesome shows, where intimate scenes were displayed as fireworks, the screen went black before the couple kissed, or the couple held their arms up covering their mouths or faces or turned from the camera. This was clean TV that could be watched by the family. As a recently baptized Believer (the second time in 2020), I am on the hunt for shows that keep me centered in a good place.

"Monica," Dad said again.

I inhaled loudly as I watched the bionic man begin to turn over a car.

"Monica, you are not made of glass!" Dad yelled.

It was now the fourth time he'd tried to get my attention to move. Yes, this was the first place I heard "you are not made of glass." I heard it on a regular basis. I couldn't write this book without including my contribution to this statement that lots of kids my age heard.

I finally moved to the side so he could see the TV. It's probably the only time I could legally ignore my dad and walk away without any repercussions. I then took a seat at the foot of the bed and finished watching the program with Dad.

I, like many, marvel at the advances in technology in our lifetime. Today, you can speak into your TV remote or call out to your voice assistant. Technology helps itself to reinvent itself. We have yet to reach the limits of artificial intelligence technology, but I guess that is the whole point. Technology continually evolves and makes things better, faster, and newer. As humans, we must remember that the continuous evolution into our tomorrow selves should never cease.

POEM
PENETRATE WALLS

Your love penetrates walls. It saw me before I saw myself. It spoke to me before I heard my voice. It imagined my future. It dreamed of me day and night, night and day. It monitored my every move. It touched my cells, my tissue, my muscles, my bones, my flesh. It shared its life with me. It shared its most sacred space. I felt your love's protection. I was safe before dawn and at dusk. Your love rocked me into its rhythm.

Your love gave me hope. It gave me a piece of its power, wisdom, and energy. Can I stay here forever? Your love creates dreams, aspirations, and can make me climb mountains, reach new heights of my evolution.

Your love diffuses the world's attacks. Your love envelops me in its purity. It never wavers, and it gets stronger each time it looks at me. Your love feels my every emotion and thought like it was its own. Your love is an unbreakable bond that will always love me. It's a gift. The strongest involuntary love imaginable. It stems from Godly love. God gave you a piece of his love, and you have passed it on to me. Your hugs are love everlasting. Your hugs are snapshots of all that we have endured. What a gift, this love that God has given us. When you see me, it's like a movie moving at triple the speed of our first encounter 'til today.

Your eyes opened bright, and you smiled. You smiled because you knew that Jesus had begun the delicate work of shaping me in your womb. You touched your tummy, connected to Holy Spirit, and said thank you. Thank you for another gift of a beautiful spirit that you have placed in a body that I will give birth to. You felt the angels celebrate because a child would be born.

You saw my future, and it was bright. The Holy Spirit gave you a peek at me, and all you saw was a smile. A smile smiling at you reflecting your love. You said I was born smiling, and when you saw me—when the doctors held me up—I smiled. I smiled because I knew I had made it. I knew your love for several months, and I could finally look in your eyes, lie on your chest, and enjoy the harmony of your love raising me, reproofing me, celebrating me, sacrificing for me, nurturing me, and being the biggest cheerleader that I would meet in my life. Thank you for your love. It was so grand and so pure that I could see it. My heart will always know your heart. We are inseparable. When I see your favorite color, lavender, I think of you. I love you and will see you when I get to heaven.

    Love you, Mommie,
Monica

CHAPTER 9
THE FOUNDATION OF THE HOUSE: GOD IS GOOD

I'VE INTRODUCED you to my dad, but of course I couldn't write this book without introducing you to my angelic mom. She was the backbone of the household and my other hero.

I was blessed to have such an angelic parent. She never missed a game or an event. Mom's smile would make a person's heart stop, and then it would resuscitate it back to life.

That smile made hurt disappear in a millisecond. It lit up my soul and my future, and I was just grateful this person standing in front of me was all mine so that I could feel this pure goodness again and again and again. How can someone just ooze so much love for everyone, not just her children?

I apparently got the smiling trait from Mom. She said I was born smiling. Pause just a second. What does that mean? Imagine all the pain and suffering my mom went through thrashing around trying to get me out of her as quickly and safely as possible. She sweated, screamed, pushed—you know how it works—and then I came out, and I was not crying? What? I had a smile on my face after enduring a several-month journey of darkness, food out of a tube, and quarters more cramped than my New York City studio in Chelsea. Maybe I was just so overjoyed it was over and the dance of life was about to begin. Now, I know I was grossly optimistic, even at birth. So naïve.

I have noticed smiling is my default expression. I read when you smile, the brain believes you are happy.

When I visited Thailand, the land of the smiling faces, I was elated that I could let loose my smiles all day, every day. Smiling is so powerful. It changes the atmosphere in an instant and a situation. My smile says I acknowledge you and pleasantly give you a gift of a piece of my positivity in this moment. It's a virtual hug.

My mom was also no-nonsense. I felt the love, but oh boy, do not—and I mean do not—break the house rules. Her reprimands were swift and just as effective as Dad's. She handled eighty percent of the reprimands and never took a day off. A violation or disobedience never slipped her grasp. I look back and feel they were a balanced parenting team. An absolute parent parure. Mom was the first line of defense, but when the offense was huge, it was escalated, and she shifted it to Dad. When that happened, I knew things were about to get real.

My mom gave me love and tenderness and my unquenchable compassion to help others, which will stay with me for a lifetime. To see family, friends, and strangers be the best they can be in every aspect of their lives comes from my mom. Her intuition was jaw-dropping. Her relationship with God was inspiring and unwavering, even in the toughest of times. Her commitment to our family, even when she worked a full-time job, was incredible. Her supernatural ability to raise a family with precision and success is worthy of nothing less than a standing ovation. Bravo, Mommie…bravo. She is my shero.

One of my mom's favorite sayings was "God is good." I heard this phrase a lot growing up from Mom and others, but I do not hear it much anymore. So, when I heard this said on a comedy show recently, it was a nice trigger of childhood memories.

Before I knew it, I laughed out loud. I was in my home office watching a comedy skit on YouTube. I was supposed to be working on a few deadlines, but my brain needed a quick reprieve.

I leaned forward in my chair toward the computer screen. This skit was hilarious and witty with subtle and not-so-subtle messages.

It takes a certain mixture of comedy to get me to laugh out loud. I tend toward the brainy comics who are incredible storytellers with an intuitive gift for timing and wit and a true connection with what entertains an audience.

The quick zingers have their place, but mix comedy with meaning, intellect, purpose, and double meanings, and I'm all ears. If a comic can make the subtlest details truly funny, that is a skill I applaud.

Okay, back to YouTube... Then I laughed out loud at the fact that I laughed out loud. I love when this happens though. It's as if I just received a comic Hershey's Kiss—surprisingly good, brief, but effective.

I can name the comedians that hit my involuntary funny button. These comics don't appear to be trying hard to be funny, they just are. It's natural, and it's a treat to watch.

Okay, let me tell you what I'm watching. It's only fair that I share. It's called *A Black Lady Sketch Show: Courtroom Kiki*. This series has some smooth skit writing for you. You must pay attention, or you might miss some of the comedy.

Did the judge ask the question "God is good?" Wow. This was her sending out the I love Jesus Believer signal to determine whether she was dealing with the same like-minded Believers. It is normally phrased as a statement, but in the comedy scene, the judge phrased it as a question, which added another layer of humor.

And an attorney, bailiff, and courtroom stenographer answered perfectly in unison, "All the time."

The skit had a happy ending with everyone singing and dancing in the courtroom. The skit was so good I watched it twice, but the "God is good" took me straight back to my childhood when landlines ruled the land and my mom had never-ending phone conversations with her friends.

Imagine late 1970s, an almond-colored landline (yes, it had a cord) on the wall next to the kitchen, and your mom being on the phone with one of her closest friends on a Saturday morning.

"Girrll, you know I needed that break," Mom said.

"It was amazing. What a blessing. After I spent three hours in the store shopping for back-to-school clothes, I got to the register, and there was my angel who voluntarily paid for my merchandise."

Shirley was one of my mom's best friends.

They spoke regularly. This was pre-cell phones and call waiting. Shirley was around my mom's age and had a son. Mom met her at our church a few times, and they just hit it off. If she liked you, she *loved* you for life.

Mom had her purse in one hand and the phone on her right shoulder as she spoke to Shirley about the monetary gift she'd received from a stranger at the store. "I'm still looking in my wallet because half my money is still in it," Mom said as she opened her wallet for the fourth time.

"God is good," Mom said in a celebratory voice and paused to hear Shirley finish the rest of the popular saying.

"All the time," Shirley said so loud I could hear her through the phone and I was a few feet away.

That's right, Shirley. You said it," Mom repeated to Shirley as she verbally emphasized *All the time*.

"I can now give some of the money I saved to Claire for her kids' school clothes. God blessed me, so I'll bless someone else.

"Let me tell you every detail of what happened. I was checking out, and Monica was saying how much she loved her orange pants, and this lady came up to me and said, 'I watched you patiently spend hours with your children as they tried on practically the entire store. I saw you calculating the total as you saw things being added to your basket, and I just wanted to bless you. I can tell the way your children behave that you are a good mother. My husband and I run a restaurant, and God has really blessed us. I just want to bless you. I don't know if you need it, but I'm doing it anyway. Now, please, take the blessing and keep raising these beautiful kids. I hope they have a great school year.'

"I just stood there and smiled at her. I didn't know what to say. She had just paid for half of our bill. I hugged her, told all the kids to say thank you, checked out, and left saying, 'God is good.' Sometimes God just wants you to know He's watching, He's with you, and just wants to give you a treat. I felt like the girls when their uncles come over and take them for ice cream." (My siblings and I had nice uncles: Uncle Kenneth regularly treated us to ice cream; Uncle William took us for ice cream/shrimp and often gave money; and Uncle Kim kept everyone laughing.)

Mom said her goodbyes and hung up the phone.

I understand it more now than I did as a child. God was always on her mind, heart, and in her conversations, and she had people in her life who clearly felt the same way. She said it with such an attitude of gratitude. As a Christian/Believer, what a beautiful childhood memory. Be mindful of what you say to or around your children because they are listening, even when they do not realize they are.

When you are speaking to your friends, when someone asks how you are doing, say, "God is good." When you are ending a conversation or giving praise, say, "God is good." I pray right now that all is well with your soul as you read these words, and I will meet you in the next chapter.

CHAPTER 10
ENTER AT YOUR OWN RISK

"ENTER AT YOUR OWN RISK" should have been plainly displayed on our back door at my childhood home. Boys had no clue what awaited them in my home.

"Don't go to the door," Mom said sternly as I eagerly awaited the next victim—I mean, boy—to exit his car. "He better get out the car." Mom parted the drapes and peeked out the living room window.

She stood on guard because she saw her daughter growing into a young woman who had to be in charge of her respect. I must command respect in order to get the best treatment was my mother's thinking. Well, actually, I should command it, but if a gentleman didn't automatically display this natural behavior, then he wasn't the one for my future.

Mom kept an eye on us, but Dad was very serious about the dating life of his children. Another one of Dad's rules was don't bring any knuckleheads home.

Dad was hard-core when it came to his daughters.

Dad had a common routine whenever I brought home a dating prospect. It actually served as a good filter because I would think ahead, knowing what the boy would have to go through, and if I did not think he could survive my dad's interrogation, I did not bother bringing him home. It also further instilled in me to have higher standards.

"No, ma'am," Omar said as he looked down at the kitchen table.

This boy was so scared after seeing my dad walk through the kitchen, he turned down Mom's pound cake. Who does that? Yes, he had never tasted it before, but any pound-cake–eating person who got a whiff of the delicate aroma that attacked you as soon as the cake saver lid was lifted would have known it was triple-A, top-shelf pound cake. I gasped out loud in a clutch-my-pearls moment. This was a serious mistake he made. Mom's pound cake could have been sold nationwide.

Thank God one of my sisters, Carla, has this cooking gene, and may God continue to bless her apron and spatula. She is keeping the pound cake and many of our family generational recipes alive. I pray she opens a restaurant soon. The world will be a better place with her food on our plates.

But wait, it did take him a long time to get the word *no* out. It seemed like he was fighting himself. He was so scared, he wasn't thinking straight. His fight or flight had kicked in, and he needed to be able to run top speed if necessary. He could not have a slice of pound cake weighing him down. I mean, it's called pound cake for a reason. Well, it looked like the fear of Dad had struck again.

A few moments earlier, I peeked out the window of our brick corner home and watched Omar GQ up the driveway. He was cute, had brains, went to church, was chill, kind, a gentleman, loved his parents, loved to watch me dance in the Top 20 dance troupe, was a great dancer, a kind alpha male, and humble.

He had a natural confidence, which was a magnet for my young heart. He rang the doorbell, and per Mom's instructions, we didn't answer the door right away. I under no circumstances could answer the door. My mom answered it, said hello, and as soon as Omar stepped in the door, Dad briskly walked past him with a pistol hanging out his back pocket.

Where did he come from? He was home? Dad had this supernatural ability to just appear. Last I saw him, he was pulling out the driveway over an hour ago, and I was happy he left because I knew I had a date coming over.

I'm telling you, parents have a radar that is unmatched by any machine man can ever make. We didn't have cell phones back then. Did Mom send up a smoke signal? How did he know?

Dad, we're only sixteen. We're just going to the matinee, I thought. I prayed this one had the courage of a lion and would tough out the initiation that was about to happen. Mom ignored Dad because Dad always attempted to intimidate boys who wanted to date me and escorted Omar to the kitchen table, where I was sitting, waiting with a million-dollar smile.

"Hi, Omar," I gushed.

"Hi, Monica." He straightened his skinny tie.

"Thank you for the beautiful poem today," I whispered under my breath.

He took a minute to look in my eyes. "I just write what I see. When I look into your eyes, I see my future. Your eyes are a precious gift to the world. And when you smile…I hear sweet heavenly music."

I blushed for what felt like two days and just smiled at him until we were interrupted *again* by Dad walking briskly by with a pistol hanging out his back pocket. This was the second time. I'm not making this up. He did this with every boy we brought home. The third time, he made eye contact with Omar briefly and kept walking. So now you can see why Omar turned down pound cake. I looked over at Omar, and the vibe was now gone. I'd be lucky if I could walk him back to his car.

He barely looked at me and kept looking at his watch. Well, I was about to see just how alpha his male was. There was a fifty-fifty chance we'd make it to the movies.

Dad was back. He appeared out of nowhere, placed his pistol on the table, and a stare-off ensued with Omar. Rather than accepting the cake Mom offered, Omar got heat—a pistol placed in front of him.

I watched, too, 'cause after all, Daddy didn't raise no punk.

Will he blink? Can he make it? Will he crumble? Does he like me enough to endure this type of date shakedown every time he comes to my house? I pondered.

As Dad stared at him, gun sitting there, he said absolutely nothing. He didn't even say hello. This was like a cop show during the interrogation scenes. My dad was literally scanning this poor boy's thoughts, intentions, future, and body language. Nice, Dad.

Success. Omar did it. Someway, somehow, he dug deep and mustered up David-like strength and struck up a conversation with my father. David is a biblical character, and I knew it would take a miracle for Omar to survive the kitchen table interview. He recognized Dad's pistol and said his older brother had the same one, and that's how it started. He was going to college, so Dad liked that, and he was a B-plus student among other positive items on this young-man-on-the-move's résumé. Unbeknownst to me, he was a crazy boxing fan. This boy started to turn into boyfriend potential right before my eyes.

All young men weren't successful in the journey to the Smith kitchen table. Some fled, never to be seen or heard from again.

―――

The last time I had a conversation with Dad about dating was in the early 2000s. Due to Dad's history, I felt obligated to seek his approval. I felt like I'd betrayed him. When I told him I was speaking to someone who was not of our race, he did not hesitate and said in a kind voice, "Monica, be with who you love."

Love is always the perfect answer. Dad was truly a winner…an overcomer. Even with all that he had been through, he still understood the importance of love.

VICTORIES

One man can make a difference. Dad fought on many fronts throughout his life, including the battlefield, the boxing ring, and the courtroom. This section takes you to the front line of these battles. A fictional story has been created around these true events to help the reader better understand these moments in my father's life.

Victory starts in the mind; once you control your mind, you will design outcomes.

CHAPTER 11
SAVED BY BOXING

AS I SAID BEFORE, the relationship with my father was really an unrelenting boot camp, which lasted until I moved out. As an African American man raising children, he raised us with precision, purpose, and a strong hand. He never took a day off from this fatherhood boot camp.

He knew it was his responsibility to prepare us. He would say, "No one is going to take their foot off your neck unless you make them" or "No one is going to take their foot off your ass unless you make them." He said these statements on autopilot. People who have been in a war know that the fight changes you forever. It changes a person's wiring, how they view their existence, their purpose, and how the forces at work in the world interplay with their very own life. They look fear in the eye daily and have thousands of conversations with it. They can smell its breath, see the color of its eyes, and read its mind. They see it coming a mile away. They know they cannot get rid of it, so the strong ones conquer it. They use its byproduct—adrenaline—as fuel to stay alive. They manipulate its code and lasso it like a bull rider at a rodeo. They rewrite its program so thinking is not impacted; it's sharpened. Reaction time is faster, breathing is more deliberate, and they recode the messages that the brain sends the muscles and the body.

"It's so dark. The wind, the wind is talking to me. I can't even hear my heart pounding in my chest. What is that?"

As bullets missed him by inches, he tried to steady his descent and his mind, which seemed to scream back at him, telling him to run from the bullets, but there was nowhere to run—at least not at the moment.

"They're trying to kill us! This is a war on Black American men! I want a family, a life!" he screamed as he felt the all-too-familiar pull of the earth on his body. He had no idea how fast he was descending, but it felt faster than it did in training. He must get the timing just right to pull the cord. He imagined he was invisible to the enemy as bullets whirled around him. He saw some of his army buddies out of the corner of his eye who were parachuting around him.

Being a boxer, you understand that fighting and survival are mental as well as physical strength. He centered his mind, held back the anger of having to leave his family behind after being drafted into service for this double war—a war on Black American men and a war with Vietnam. He was parachuting behind enemy lines, and if the Vietnamese didn't kill him, he had to also watch out for the white, racist American soldiers.

At least I'm parachuting with some of my Black buddies. We have a pact that we'll watch each other's backs against the racist American soldiers who start fights and randomly decide when they want to have target practice and shoot a Black man, he said to himself.

I wonder what the Stars and Stripes meant to my dad since he was drafted into the war. The Vietnam War was the first to integrate Blacks and whites. He trained at Fort Campbell, Kentucky, and entered the 506th Infantry, 101st Airborne unit as a paratrooper.

I recently found out he was in the war. He never told me or my siblings. In fact, I remember I asked him…twice. I can understand why he didn't tell me. Who wants to recount those memories over and over? Had I known, I have no doubt I would have asked a deluge of questions that would have only tapered off once I got old enough to realize that it would be best to leave war where it belongs, in the history books. It also would have brought great sadness to his children and the family to know what he endured.

Yes. This was Dad. Always kept up a strong exterior and didn't let anyone take his peace of mind and happiness. It was the right choice as far as the children, but I do hope he had an outlet to discuss when he needed.

Dad had two nicknames, Smitty and Butch, because of the royal beatdowns he delivered in the boxing ring. If he were alive today, since I speak Smitty, I'm guessing he would say this about the war:

"How can a man assume the role of God and decide who will live or die in their chess game for their benefit and gain?

"Men were forced to kill in another man's war. Young men were sent to die with no lineage to leave behind. Millions of bloodlines vanished in thin air. Their blood stained the soil in a strange land they could not call home.

"Unfulfilled dreams with no guide to escort them to their rightful future. Legacies were left stranded. They died in fear, the worst way to die. May God bless their souls. Many prayers went up to heaven for a safe return, and many never made it back. Great friendships were built among the men, but what is a friendship when you are living the future second by second? What type of friendship is it when you must pray for the friend just as much as yourself on a minute-by-minute basis?

"Many people, thankfully, will never understand the feeling of an unending adrenaline rush. The necessity to stay alert even in your sleep. Most people will never understand the feeling of being forced to do something against your will that will likely kill you. With no apologies, no thank you.

"Every man drafted should have been able to live free the rest of his life. His family should have received significant benefits for the trauma the soldier brought home and how it would impact the household. A life for a life. If the government wanted to force me to risk my life, they should have offered to completely take care of me for life. It was a one-sided deal where the dealer did not know your name. You were just a number, a card in the deck. Praying your card was never played.

"It was the purest form of madness in a madman's puppet show."

I wish I'd given Dad more hugs.

I think about all these young men ripped out of their lives and forced to fight in terrain and conditions and with people they know nothing about. My community lost generations of men and women who could have been born to the lost soldiers. The elders of the community tell me it became a generational genocide, which devastated the community, and many of the ones who did make it out alive were damaged for life. If the easily obtainable and abundant supply of drugs did not get them, Agent Orange—or the unfriendly friendly fire—did.

I was also told separate needles were not used when they vaccinated the troops. They lined men up and vaccinated them with the same needle. Men who were blessed enough to return home brought back illnesses and diseases they did not have before they departed for the war. Of course, sharing needles is no longer done today.

Dad would take his boxing skills to Vietnam and box his comrades. It was an outlet in many ways. I imagine the conversations went something like this:

"Where's Butch?" yelled the sergeant to whoever was in hearing distance.

"You mean Smitty?" one of the soldiers asked inquisitively.

"Verdell, Butch, Smitty… Whatever name he's going by today. Where is he?"

"Well, sir, we call him Butch when he's boxing and Smitty when he's not," the soldier said to the sergeant.

A fellow soldier and friend of Dad's yelled, "He's over there sparring with Leroy! I think someone needs to save Leroy—and quick! He doesn't stand a chance with Butch!"

The sergeant walked over and watched Dad throw a multitude of combination punches with turbo-like speed. Each punch connected, and Leroy was out. As usual, all his fights ended in a knockout.

"Butch, now that you've sent Leroy for his afternoon nap, come over here for a moment," said the sergeant, shaking his head as he looked down at Leroy. "Butch, the enemy is knocking men out. We don't need you doing it too. I need the men sharp and ready, not battered and bruised," he said under his breath.

"Yes, sir," Dad said as he exited killer mode.

He stuck out his right hand and then his left toward someone in the crowd watching, and they unlaced his gloves. He tied them together and swung his gloves over his shoulders. Like a ship captain to his compass, he knew where his gloves were always.

"Smith, may I call you by your proper army name now since you're not in the ring?" asked the sergeant in a sarcastic manner. "Word has gotten to the right people that you know how to box. We're sending you back to the States to box for the army. You'll travel the country, and it'll be better than staying in this wretched jungle. Today is your lucky day. Grab your belongings, and you leave at 0500 tomorrow."

"Sir, I don't know who made this decision, but I just want to say thank you if you made the call," Dad said.

"You belong in the ring—heck, you belong in the international ring. Nobody survives your hand-to-hand combat—at least not in one piece," the sergeant acknowledged as he looked grateful that Dad would get an opportunity to continue a boxing career.

Dad saluted the sergeant and went to prepare for his early morning departure.

I knew from a very young age that my father was a boxer. Now, my father was born in the 1940s, which means he was boxing in the sixties. Back then, boxers fought all classes. He fought across weight classes and emerged as the number one boxer in the army. He won every fight by knockout. We have pictures of him, standing at five feet, six inches, with his arm raised with his opponent over six feet, dozens of pounds heavier, and asleep from the symphonic and bionic combination punches he'd just received from Dad.

It just so happened that I began this book around the time Muhammad Ali passed. He and Dad were born in the same year. They each boxed in the 1960s, and I recall Dad mentioned he had met him. Dad was drafted and served several years prior to Ali's draft date. Boxing was the means for Dad to get out of war-torn Vietnam. Boxing could have very well saved his life. Praise God.

Think about how good one must be to beat army men. They train all day in real time and learn combat that is the difference between life and death. This is a completely different level of boxing ability. He put a stamp on his title. Below is what we believe could be a picture of Dad winning the All-Army Boxing Championship, but then again, he won every fight by knockout, so who knows? Dad was 150 pounds while in the army so he would have likely been in either the light middleweight or welterweight categories.

In the picture, he is standing in the middle of the ring, gloves on, satin shorts with the Screaming Eagles 101st Airborne emblem and protective headgear or face saver, and the referee holds up his right hand signaling he is the champ. A satin cloak drapes his shoulders as the bright lights illuminate the ring against the pitch-black backdrop of the room. He looks like a pure muscle, world-class boxing machine. Even the referee looks famous.

One of my siblings also recently found a handwritten note of someone in the army congratulating him for his win. It looks like someone in a leadership role wrote the note and listed the other boxers who came in second, third, and fourth place.

He left the army but not before turning down an opportunity to box in the Olympics. (He sometimes reminisced about this lost opportunity.) He settled down with my mom, went to work at the mill, and he had no idea he was about to enter another fight for his life, a fight in the judiciary system.

Winning Boxing Match (Photo Credit – US Army)

Dear Reader,

As I researched my dad's military record, I reviewed his DD 214 and was surprised when I did not see Vietnam/foreign service listed. This prompted me to do some digging, and I discovered that it is not totally uncommon for some Vietnam Veterans' DD 214s to not reflect their service in Vietnam.

The government provides the opportunity to submit a request for the records to be corrected, but this still may not always result in correction. Based on research, there are different reasons someone's record may be incorrect. Apparently, government recordkeeping and tracking became more accurate later in the war. My dad was drafted in the earlier years of the war. I read that one reason could be if a soldier was on a special mission/special operation (which could be the case for my dad, considering his missions and his infantry/division), the records would have been considered confidential and sealed.

Someone my dad knows very well shared with me a few years ago that Dad told him he was in Vietnam and was dropped behind enemy lines. He also told this person, they pulled him out because he could box.

When I was a child, I asked Dad if he was in the war. He looked caught off guard, immediately averted his eyes, and walked away. The second time I asked, he did a double take and was clearly surprised I asked this question. He mumbled something under his breath, averted his eyes, and again walked away. As a child, I took this as his answer must be "no," but now looking through an adult lens, this was clearly an "I don't want to talk about it" response.

I also learned from the wife of a Vietnam veteran that some of the vets were spit on when they returned to the States. This just further confirms why Dad clearly did not want to talk about it.

It's a bleeding wound in world history, and we pray it never happens again. May God bless and heal all those directly and indirectly impacted. May He rip its grip of pain, misery, and memories from those who were there. May He loose peace, conscious and subconscious mental freedom, and physical and spiritual wholeness in every way on those who were there, their families and their offspring. May He remove any generational imprints and send a stream of Christ-anointed joy, healing, purification, and love through their bloodlines. In Jesus's name. Amen.

And I will give unto thee the keys of the kingdom of heaven: and whatsoever thou shalt bind on earth shall be bound in heaven: and whatsoever thou shalt loose on earth shall be loosed in heaven (Matthew 16:19 KJV).

I do not proclaim to be an expert on Vietnam or war or a military researcher.

I have a sincere respect for all those who have served in the military and the families they left behind. We thank you for your service, and may God continue to bless you and your family.

CHAPTER 12
PAPERS, PAPERS, PAPERS

FLASHBACK. There it was again. Flashback. I walked into my living room in an Atlanta suburb in May 2020. I had papers scattered on the floor as I organized them to file away, and it was like a movie just started to play in my head.

What is that? How could Papers, Papers, Papers trigger such a potent memory unlock? I said to myself. I stopped and looked around my living room like I'd never seen it before because I saw my living room but also my childhood home in the same moment. Believe it or not, one of my most vivid memories of my childhood is of papers scattered on the basement floor of my home.

"Don't walk on the papers!" Dad blurted out as I turned to the right and entered the pool table side of our basement and stepped half of my right foot onto an innocent large envelope on the floor. It is the late 1970s, and I heard this directive many times growing up.

"Oops. Sorry, Dad," I immediately apologized.

"Watch where you are going," he said sternly as he looked up and watched where I was about to place my next footstep.

"Okay," I immediately said as I began to gather the balls to play a game of pool. It was too hot to be outside, so I'd come downstairs to choose from pool, darts, dancing, TV, video games, or listen to music.

The basement had two sides, divided by the recessed stairway that was painted a dark gray. Dad and his papers were always on the side with the pool table. He personally finished the basement, and it was of professional caliber. He was a perfectionist and certainly could have run a construction company. The flooring on this side was two-by-two white-and-black checkers to reflect that it was game time. He would later teach me how to play pool, checkers, and Ping-Pong. I must say, playing pool did come in handy on a date or two when I was an adult. And, of course, there was the infamous chess table where, unbeknownst to me, Dad taught me my first life lessons and strategy. Learning chess was mandatory in our home, and he studied my skill level each time we played. He offered guidance, but I never beat him.

Dad organized his papers on the floor, which did not look organized at all—too many papers to count. We just tried not to walk on them. These papers were stationary pieces of furniture on the basement floor and were there because Dad embarked on the impossible: he filed a lawsuit against the Globalwest Steel on Second Lake. Mom was right there supporting him, being a strategic sounding board and typing hundreds of documents. The lawsuit spanned more than ten years of my childhood.

I partially knew what was happening. My life's work at the time was running around in pigtails mastering my roundabout, cartwheel, and double Dutch skills.

I remember this lawsuit was serious business though. How dare this man go against the behemoth Globalwest? What guts, what courage, what moxie to fight to make them accountable. He needed to fight for his dignity and the soul of justice.

After I played a game of pool, I walked to the other side of the basement and turned on the Atari video console. As I played *Asteroids*, I overheard Mom ask Dad what time his meeting was the next day with his attorneys. He told her 11:00 a.m.

He was battling a giant manufacturer, and I was saving my spaceship from giant rocks in outer space. I had to hit them multiple times to break them into pieces, then destroy the pieces. Indeed, the smaller asteroids could be considered more dangerous—faster, harder to see, and harder to avoid.

Although the large, lumbering rocks presented a different challenge—they often lulled one into a false sense of safety—approaching your ship quicker and closer than their initially perceived vector would indicate, once the large rocks were obliterated, there was just no predicting what paths their offspring detritus would take.

Asteroid connoisseurs will tell you that hitting the larger rocks truly required skill. Fire too soon, and the pieces scattered far and wide, perhaps irretrievably so. Fire too close, and the asteroid could blow up too close to your ship. And in case you misjudged, thank goodness for hyperspace!

The only guaranteed constant in the game was the math. One craggy missile broke into two, two broke into four, and four broke into eight. Although just a game, my adult analysis prompts the following insights:

- Smaller asteroids can still kill, so never underestimate the size or power of your opponent. Dad, who stood at five feet, six inches, certainly proved that to be true.
- Division can be the destruction of the larger plan or destruction of the source of power or destruction can be a collective group of adversaries. *Divide and conquer.*
- To win, sometimes you must keep hitting and *leave no crumbs...* or small asteroids. Some adversaries you can knock out with one punch, while other fights may go the distance. Think twelve to fifteen rounds in boxing.

I played *Asteroids* for a few hours, turned the game off, then walked into the laundry room to iron my clothes for school the next day.

. . .

Always remember, *leave no crumbs.*

CHAPTER 13
SUCCESS IS THE ONLY OPTION

IT WAS a stormy day at 10:35 a.m. on a Tuesday. Dad was early for his 11:00 a.m. meeting with his attorneys. It was supposed to be spring, but winter didn't receive the memo. It was as if the weather knew the events that were to transpire.

Dad parked his car in the parking lot of the twenty-floor brown office building. He finished his cold cup of coffee, grabbed his dark brown briefcase, opened it up, and took a quick look to ensure he had brought the proper paperwork. He opened it again and decided to review the contract one more time, ensuring he had the legal right to execute the conversation he was walking into. He put on his business face, mentally reviewed the countless reasons he'd made this decision, and exited his car.

He entered the lobby and scrolled down the list of companies in the building. He knew where he was going but just wanted to make sure. He entered the elevator and pushed the third floor. He played out the conversation in his head and his responses to their expected rejection of his position. His plan moving forward was well thought out and solid. He entered the high-end offices of his attorneys ready to get this conversation behind him.

"Mr. Smith, just wait a second here. We've worked with you for years. We're doing what we can. We've spent hundreds of hours on your case and don't want things to end this way. Hey, man, we're on your side. Really, you've got to trust us here—" Dad's attorney pleaded.

"That's my point. I don't see a clear path to success with the way things are unfolding. You won't need to spend any more time on this matter. I'm canceling my contract. Success is the only option. Winning is the only option. If you don't see the win, taste the win, smell the win, and want to win, then it won't happen. I have a case, they're guilty, and the facts are irrefutable. I'm treating this case like Muhammad Ali versus Joe Frazier, and you're treating it like a sparring session with Ronald McDonald," Dad said, not raising his tone or changing his relaxed-on-a-Sunday-afternoon posture.

There was no way they would beat him in the battle of communication. They may have had their law degrees, but he had been in the ring too many times with real-life giants and on a real battlefield. He understood human behavior and deception way too much to be outdone.

Dad decided to try his own case against Globalwest for the loss of part of his right leg when the crane that he was coerced to drive blew up shortly after he sat in it. He disbanded his army of lawyers and courageously read and proceeded to educate himself on the law and the complex United States judicial system. He suspected his lawyers were attempting to sabotage his case, a classic double agent maneuver. He fought his case like David versus Goliath. *Ding! Ding! Ding!* Sounds the bell at the start of the match.

In my opinion, he had already won at this point. Standing up or taking the first step can be just as hard if not harder than winning. Think about the force needed to get a large boat to move, but once it gets going, it can more easily pick up speed and enter cruise control. I'm by no means minimizing winning; I'm just clarifying that fighting the urge to be complacent and making the first step is in a separate battle and the first battle to be won. The first step breaks off the chains of fear. It is the most powerful step in a fight and many times determines the outcome. This is why the element of surprise has been used in numerous fights and encounters.

What a tremendously brave decision to represent himself in his lawsuit. This was typical for Dad. Courage ran through his veins. Being in the commercial retail real estate industry and negotiating hundreds of deals in forty-seven states, I regularly encounter legal contracts and negotiation. As I look at his monumental decision, pre-internet, no college degree, and no attorney friends or family to call, it leaves me speechless. He did all this being injured, while raising a large family and working. He is my hero, and I must also honor my mom for being his staunch partner.

BUT—and this is a big *but*—he unfortunately had no idea the minefield of deception that would come his way during the lawsuit. As you will see in the next chapter, he learned there was another enemy among him…in his very own camp.

CHAPTER 14
TURNCOATS

"YOU WILL NEED to hurry up and eat. We have company coming over soon, and I need y'all to go in the basement or outside," Mom ordered.

Jazz played in the background on a replica of a 1930s radio. Mom loved jazz, and it was always floating through the air in the kitchen. It's the late 1970s, and even as a young child, not quite ten years old yet, I still welcomed its soothing and intelligent rhythms. I knew it was good music, even though I wouldn't fully understand its complexity, history, and necessity in the African American community until I got older.

"Who's coming over?" I asked.

"Some of your dad's friends from work."

I grabbed a plate and fork and set it at my assigned seat at the kitchen table. Dinner was not ready yet, but I wanted my plate to be.

"Oh, I see you're always at the table when it's roast, but I can't pay you to eat vegetables," Mom said.

"But I love roast. Did you make creamed corn too?"

"Yes, and don't forget to throw the potato skins in the garbage."

Earlier, I'd peeled the potatoes quickly but carefully. This was one of my favorite meals: roast, creamed corn, and homemade mashed potatoes. I remember peeling potato after potato after potato growing up.

"So glad we have a sparkling floor. Thanks for scrubbing the floor last night."

"You're welcome," I replied.

At eleven, the night before, I was dragging a grouchy bucketful of Pine-Sol and a dash of Dawn while my young knees made their way through the kitchen and bathroom as I meticulously scrubbed every square inch.

Yup, we scrubbed floors back then. The floors looked amazing afterward, but boy, it was a lot of work.

I admit, sometimes I look at my floors and say, *Boy, it would be great if you could get a good scrubbing, but not by me and not today* as I pull out the mop, grateful I am an adult.

I finished my meal, grabbed a grape Popsicle, exited stage left—or out the back door—leaped off the top concrete stair, twisted in the air, and landed a perfect 10 on the concrete with the Popsicle safely intact. Boy, I was good. I peeled back the wrapper and watched its demise slowly unfold before my eyes. I loved everything grape—grape Kool-Aid, grape Now and Laters, grape juice, grape Jolly Ranchers, grape Life Savers, and of course…grapes.

A dark brown car pulled up at the curb next to our house, and a couple got out. It was Melinda and Leroy. Leroy was Dad's coworker and Melinda was his wife. I recognized Melinda because she always took time to speak to me and asked about my grades. She was the first person who told me about Spelman College. Another car pulled up behind them, and it was another of Dad's coworkers who had been at our house before. They waved at me; I waved back, then turned my attention to my quickly fleeting ice on a stick, which I was showing no mercy.

• • •

Leroy and Melinda's house before they left for Butch and Brenda's house for dinner... (What follows is how I imagine their conversation went.)

"Baby, you ready to head over to Brenda and Butch's house for dinner?" Leroy asked Melinda as he passed through their home kitchen. They lived on the other side of E.C.

Melinda grabbed her special occasion teal blue cake saver with the crystal ornament on top and gently placed the German chocolate cake she'd baked inside. She used the family's beloved recipe from her great-grandmother in Arkansas.

"Cake is done. I just have to check my face again and grab my shoes." She walked toward the bathroom to apply her makeup, avoiding eye contact with Leroy.

Leroy walked past in a hurry, obviously feeling nervous and guilty for what was about to transpire. Melinda was acting distant, and it made him more tense.

Leroy walked quietly into the bathroom after her. "You are talking to me, but you *aren't* talking to me? I need to do this. There will be a financial benefit for us. I won't ever have to worry about job security at Globalwest again..."

Melinda quickly put her head down to avoid the hypnotic power of the deepest brown eyes she had ever met. They were in fact the reason she'd married him, and he knew it. She got lost in them if she looked too long.

"So that's what they told you?" she replied, looking down at the sink, then into the sunburst mirror on the wall to her left, pretending to look closely at her makeup.

How could he do this after hearing all the stories firsthand about my family escaping the South in the 1930s, leaving behind their land—how my family has a history of risking their lives to save others and to support the community?

"Leroy, I'm ready but not willing. I'll meet you outside. The name is Melinda, not Baby," she blurted out as she grabbed her fan, which matched her dress.

Leroy opened the passenger-side door, grabbed the cake, and watched the love of his life nestle into her seat. He placed the cake on her lap on top of her lap scarf.

"Why are you wearing the black outfit you only wear to funerals?" he said with a raised voice as he took a good look at what she wore and realized he only saw this dress when it was time to mourn.

After Leroy and Melinda arrived at the Smith residence...

Melinda walked in, took one look at Butch's wife's smiling face and prepared table, and felt nauseous.

I can't do this, she said to herself. *This goes against God and my family history and upbringing.*

"I'm gonna drive myself home. I'm not feeling well. Ask Butch to take you home."

Although, wow, he will have no idea that he is chauffeuring a traitor. Melinda looked disgusted and left out the back door of the Smith residence.

"She's pregnant—hasn't told anyone yet. Maybe she just needs some fresh air," Leroy said to my mom as he exited the back door.

Melinda spun around to speak to Leroy. "You are behaving like a treacherous traitor! How could I have married someone like you when I was taught about our history practically every Sunday at the dinner table? And your seed is living inside me. I'll raise this child right. He will not be weak. He will not, he will not, he will not trade his dignity for the destruction of another.

"This is a crime against me, your unborn child, and our people. Why can't you just stay out of it? Why can't you just say to Butch, 'I will not join you on this fight'? This man almost died when that crane blew up. He has a family. He is trying to help you and me by bringing you into the lawsuit. You don't see that what you're doing is stone-cold crazy, house negro textbook stuff?"

Melinda walked over to the baby apple tree so they would be hidden and could speak freely. "Oh, these look ripe and ready to eat," she said, grabbing a few baby apples for later.

"...can't back out now. If I do, I'd lose my job because they'd be afraid I'll tell Butch," he said as he tried to control his quavering voice.

"Are you the only one sidestepping your responsibility to the race? Are you the only one? Are you? Who else is a double agent? My dad is a Howard graduate, my mom a Spelman graduate, and I could not even imagine... I can't even tell them. They would be alarmed at the disease of deception, greed, no self-respect or love for your own race. You hurt yourself, too, you know? That's what I'm so surprised you don't understand. You are not who I thought I married. You portrayed a different person and life plan. I'm sending you back to the flea market for a refund. I want every cent of my money back. If you continue to try to wreck Butch's lawsuit, I will move in with my mother. You will not poison my child with your mutated mind."

"Just come back inside. You see Brenda cooked enough for two Thanksgiving dinners," Leroy pleaded.

Melinda shut the heavy car door as loud as she could, turned the key, checked her mirrors, and drove off, leaving Leroy to explain to the Smiths why his wife left.

Melinda drove home and cried because she knew Leroy was making a big mistake that would have an exponential impact on their family, as well as hers. She called her mother as soon as she walked in the door.

"How did the dinner go? I know her cooking was divine. Wish you could have brought me a plate," Melinda's mother said as soon as she answered the phone.

"You were right. I should have spent more time getting to know him before marrying him," Melinda confessed.

After Melinda left, Leroy composed himself, looked up at the apple tree he and Melinda stood under, and tasted an apple. "Man, these are some good apples," he said as he grabbed a few more, stuffed them in his pocket, then shamefully and slowly walked back into the Smith residence. He would have to keep up the lie without his wife.

"Leroy, is that an apple coming out of your pocket?" Dad laughed. "You'd better not let Monica and Gabrielle see you. They would be very angry. Those are their apples out there. Where is Melinda?"

Everyone sat down to eat what felt like Thanksgiving in July. Leroy kept his secret hidden, had seconds, and prepared a plate for Melinda.

Dad gave him a ride home after the meal. They said their goodbyes, and Leroy walked into his home, entered his living room, and saw his pillow and blankets on the couch.

"It's gonna be a long pregnancy," he huffed out loud.

After Dad drove Leroy home…

"Turncoats! Turncoats! Turncoats!" Dad yelled. "First my attorneys, now my coworkers!?" he continued as he stared at Mom in disgust and disbelief. I'd just come back in the house from riding my skateboard, and Dad had just returned from taking Leroy home.

"I can't believe it. All those dinners I served them. They sat at our table, breaking bread with us. God doesn't like a false witness, and they will be held accountable," Mom said as she cleaned the dishes and looked at the plates like she wanted to throw them away since the turncoats ate from them.

"Turncoats. Madness," Dad continued. "…And that jive turkey Leroy had me take him home. I should have dropped him off on Cline Avenue and told him to walk home. He's a low-down dirty louche, and as bad as they come.

"Were they ever sincere? Were they ever really going to testify? We have got to get this crabs-in-a-barrel disease out of the minds of our people and the community. It's like a Trojan horse. They listened to my strategy. They are trying to destroy the entire class action lawsuit. We have a case. We have a damn good case. I'm suing for me, but also for him and the other Black workers at the plant. Why would he fight this? It's for his safety too. Madness!"

"Your brother told you not to go class action. I know you wanted to help our people, but you have to help yourself first," Mom said in that I-told-you-so tone.

"What do we have to do to cut this poison out of the minds of our people? It's psychological warfare. It was done during slavery and continues today. How do we destroy betrayal? These people are a triple threat—a threat to themselves, the other Blacks involved, and a threat to the community. How do you free the mentally enslaved mind? How do we expose this parasitic divide and incinerate it from the community? It's just plain dumb. It's suicide," Dad said as if he were speaking at a podium in front of thousands.

"It's spiritual warfare. This is why Black people prayed in church and in the fields. They addressed the spirit of racism, which is the root of the problem," Mom said. "This spirit causes Blacks to turn on each other out of fear, jealousy, and self-hate imposed on them by outside forces…their enemy."

"They were shuckin' and jivin' and skinnin' and grinnin', saying 'yes, we're with you, Butch. We're going to win this thing,' only to chicken out at the last minute. Why didn't they just say no, we want no part of it? That's what I don't understand.

"I wonder how much they were paid. They set us back years. We could have helped the working conditions for the next generation of Blacks. Their children will likely work at this factory. It's just madness.

"Now that I think of it, one of them got invited over to one of the white manager's homes for dinner. I bet he was the ringleader."

Dad grabbed another piece of German chocolate cake.

"I could have just helped myself, but I couldn't stand to watch how they were being treated. Black lives were in danger every day at the plant. It was a factory Russian roulette. It was so dangerous, honey. I knew I had to do it. I couldn't have lived with myself if I hadn't. I've been to some of these guys' homes. I've met their families, seen the pride when their kids graduated from high school and got an A on their tests. I've seen the exhaustion mixed with fear as they toil away in this industrial cotton field," Dad said as he confirmed his decision to himself.

"There's a smaller percentage of us fighting for the rest of the race. You have the fight in you, so don't change that. We need you. I'm sure your efforts weren't all in vain, and you did fight your individual lawsuit. Let's not forget that. I'm sure some changes will happen, even if it's five years from now—ten years from now. This kind of change doesn't happen overnight. Your children and your children's children will know what you did. Your name will be known nationally one day. Maybe not now, maybe not in ten years, but your name will be known," Mom said.

"Honey, you know I didn't do it for that. Right is right and wrong is wrong, and I did it because all humans deserve to live and be treated like humans. A man should not act or respond as a slave. God created all equal, so we must conduct ourselves as such. Nobody can decide and self-appoint themselves as superior."

"Racism is idolatry. Their desire to be treated better than or be number one is a clear sin and in the Ten Commandments. Anyone who wants to be idolized or idolizes another, it's a big no-no," she said. "Not to mention, don't people realize what they do, good or bad, impacts their children and their bloodline? It's biblical!"

"You can't have a number one without a number two." Dad put up one finger and then two fingers.

"What they tried to do to me at that plant was a factory lynching, plain and simple. It's a miracle I survived that crane explosion and with my brain still in my head. If I lived in the South, that's exactly what would have happened. Actually, if I was little farther south in Indiana, that's what they would have tried." He headed to the table for some more pineapple 7-Up punch to wash down the cake.

"Glory be to God that your life was spared, and we have wonderful children who will see how their mother and father fought with their bare hands and prayer."

Mom finished the dishes, swept the floor, and prayed through the entire house to remove any memory or remnants of the traitors being in her home.

She thanked God that while Dad took Leroy home, Melinda called and told her that Leroy and a few other coworkers took all Dad's plans back to management, and they were going to back out of the class action case at the last minute. The court date was already set so it might be too late for the class action lawsuit, but at least Dad knew the plan.

CHAPTER 15
APPROACHING THE MOUNTAIN

"YOU HAVEN'T SMOKED in months. Keep it up." Mom walked past Dad as she stopped at the trash can and threw away yet another ashtray a few weeks prior to his court date. "I didn't realize how many ashtrays were laying around the house. Feels good to throw them out. Now their presence and the reminder of the destruction they cause and their remnants are G-O-N-E. How does it feel to have your lungs back?"

"I'm over the hardest part. The cravings are minimal now." He looked at Mom with a serious expression as he walked past her in the kitchen. He had just finished his daily regular exercise routine, which included a thousand sit-ups. "I should have done this a long time ago," he said. "My body feels more alive. I'm walking up the stairs better. My mind is getting clearer. I must train like I did for a boxing match because I'm about to enter the biggest ring of my life—the courtroom. Need to make sure my mind and body can operate in unison as they are meant."

"You will win. I know you will," Mom said as she sealed the garbage bag shut that she placed several ashtrays in.

"By the way, your Rally for the Win party is all set for this Wednesday. I am headed to the grocery store now," she said on her way out the garage door with the garbage bag of ashtrays in her hand.

Dad had done an about-face, and cigarettes and alcohol were in his crosshairs. I watched him for years take long drags on those cigarettes, which would make his entire body contract. It must be good if Dad was doing it, so I wanted to try it—or so I thought.

―――――

"Daddy, Daddy, Daddy, Daddy, Daddy," I said in my nagging little girl voice.

"What?" Dad asked.

"Can I try it?" I asked so fast it sounded like one long word rather than four.

Of course, he completely ignored my question without even looking my way while he focused on the television.

"Daddy, Daddy, Daddeeeeee, Daaaddddeeeeeee, can I try it?" I let out a tortuous tone. I had asked to smoke a cigarette for months and was tired of being ignored.

Why is he not sharing? I thought. *I'm his daughter, and he has several more in the box.*

"Dadddeee, I want to try it."

Dad suddenly looked directly at me. He had had it. He was annoyed and saw that I was not going away. I was a child. There was no job for me to go to, and it was summer break, so I had nothing but time on my hands. He'd better let me try that cigarette, or he wouldn't be able to watch TV.

His look was intense, and it was one of those moments when a parent thinks, *Ohhhh myyyy goooddnnesss, theessee kids are driving me to rethink my life decisions.*

I was maybe seven years old. He abruptly handed me the cigarette while I was still in mid-sentence putting on my best begging performance.

I stopped and looked shocked. *Is he serious?* I thought.

He said it again, "Here," and continued. "Take it."

I could barely contain my smile, and my taste buds began to do back flips. Success. I had worn him down. I immediately grabbed it before he changed his mind.

I put it in my mouth, and nothing happened.

I looked at him, disappointed, and said, "Nothing happened."

He told me to inhale. I tried again and nothing. Now I was frustrated and felt tricked.

I was growing impatient, and I looked at him again with a why-is-this-not-working look. He was now beyond his point of patience and probably had completely lost the desire to smoke for the rest of the day.

Finally, he said, "Open your mouth" and he slowly blew the smoke in my mouth, and I think I partially inhaled.

Hello. Goodbye. Where am I? I thought I was going to die on the spot. I choked for I don't know how long and never, never, never—I mean never—asked again.

When I saw cigarettes, I went the other way. He could have those trash can sticks. Enjoy. Why would he do such a thing? It was absolutely disgusting. They tasted worse than punishment.

He knew I would have this response and that there was no way a little girl would like the taste of nicotine. It's so interesting the way parents raise children over the decades and how different cultures do it. It should be noted that this childhood event deterred me from a life of cigarettes—I see them and get flashbacks.

I remember when the entire family ganged up on Dad with a stop smoking campaign. We hid his cigarettes and put up a big poster in my parents' bedroom above the TV that said it caused cancer so he could wake up to it every morning. We harassed him day and night and every time he lit up. There was nowhere in the house he could hide—or so we thought. Some of my bolder siblings lived on the edge and threw the cigarettes away, so Dad found a way to smoke under the radar and in peace. We found out one day that it was Dad who was getting the last laugh.

"I'm looking for Dad," Gabrielle said while she walked through the house.

I was sitting at the kitchen table at the time, which was next to the garage door, having a standoff with the vegetables on my plate that were getting colder by the minute. I was on a constant strike against canned green beans.

"He was here, and I didn't hear the garage door go up," Gabrielle replied, looking confused.

A family fugitive hunt ensued, and he was nowhere to be found.

Mom checked to see if his car was there since no one could find him. When she opened the garage door, he stood near the stairs like a deer in headlights with a half-smoked cigarette in his hand. It was a cold winter day, and he only had on a short-sleeved T-shirt and slacks. We had been tricked. He was still smoking! He'd been found, and the hunt was over.

"Verdell, it's freezing out there! What is that in your hand? Have you been coming out here the entire time?" Mom said to Dad, clearly shocked for several reasons.

We don't know how long he was sneaking into the attached garage for a quick smoke. The good news was our campaign still worked because it at least minimized the number of cigarettes he smoked, and he had to imagine his children's cute faces every time he lit up.

Dad also deterred me from alcohol. What is it with the way people casually hold a drink in their hand, taking such innocent sips on what appears to be a gentle drink that is soothing their senses?

Dad was in the basement enjoying his abundant album and eight-track collection and sipping on a nightcap. I was a late-night person, as was Dad. I saw him enjoying a colored beverage in a plastic cup. I planned my approach and casually asked Dad for a taste like I was asking him for grape Kool-Aid. He ignored me of course, but my persuasiveness was unrelenting, and I was getting better at it (smile). I begged and begged, and he finally gave me the cup that had a little bit of alcohol left. I took a sip, and it went straight to my head and through my body. It was so disgusting I couldn't understand why he would voluntarily drink this liquid. Was he on punishment? It was like drinking castor oil for kicks. I had a buzz from one sip.

So, Dad did what any loving father would do after his young daughter's first encounter with alcohol: we went to White Castle for some late-night burgers.

Later, in my twenties, I came to realize I had no tolerance for alcohol, so my dad's rules—and there were many—of do not smoke and do not drink were easily attainable for me. He knew there was no way a little girl would like the taste of cigarettes and alcohol, so it kept me away for life.

Also, children and adults want what they can't have. When they finally get what they've been after or chasing, many times they realize:

1. It's not good after all.
2. It's not for them.
3. They are better off without it.
4. The grass is not greener.
5. They should be careful what they wish for.
6. When something is hard to get, it may mean they aren't supposed to have it.
7. Sometimes they should accept God's protection of not getting what they wanted but will later get what they need.

Can I get an amen?

…getting back to Dad's party.

It's Wednesday, and the "Rally for the Win" day (for Dad's mill lawsuit court date) arrived, and the food was prepared an hour before the guests arrived. The house was cleaned top to bottom and there was not an ashtray to be found. Dad was not interested in a party, but Mom did it because she thought it important to have a celebratory atmosphere in the house before Dad entered court. Only people who knew about the case were invited, so that meant close family and a few of Mom's friends.

"Is Mary coming?" Mom asked expectantly.

Mary lived two blocks over. She was around seven years younger than Mom and had a boy and a girl. Her husband was on the school board. Mary was positive and polite with the perfect posture at all times. Mom was a magnet for positive thinkers.

"Yes, and we're waiting on two more people. Ten people have arrived, and I served them punch already, so don't worry yourself," said Shirley, Mom's best buddy.

My mom had done it. She had prepared for World War III. She had typed her fingers to the bone and had been Dad's secret weapon for years. She had called in reinforcements—the ultimate in prayer warriors. Seven elders from the church, her pastor, and a few family members and friends were at our house to join in prayer.

The power of prayer is unmatched, especially considering the promises God made to His children, in Jesus's name.

I watched in awe as I peeked around the corner as women and men dressed in their Sunday best sipped on punch made with fresh fruit and laced with 7-Up and nibbled on red velvet cake. Most had finished scrubbing their plates clean after eating Mom's lusciously layered lasagna. Now it appeared everyone was having a moment of silence as they devoured their slices of cake like no one was watching.

"Come here. It's so good to see you. You look so pretty, and you are so smart," Grandma—or Mommer as we called my maternal grandmother—said every time she saw me and my siblings.

"Mommmeerr," I yelled out with glee and ran over to her and happily received her hug. After the long, happy hug that only a grandparent could give, I immediately got in position and prepared for the loving critique that came at the beginning of every visit with her.

"Look at you," she said as she smiled.

I stood there while she looked me up and down. I turned around so she could see all the growing up I had done since she saw me last. She complimented me and gave me so much love. I will never forget, she always told me I was pretty *and* smart in the same sentence. Adding the word *smart* in her greeting also reinforced the way I was raised at home. Intelligence and success were the top priority.

Before we left to head to Mommer's house to continue the party, I passed through the basement and heard, "There you go." *Jab, step left. Huuhh, huhhh.*

These were the noises Dad made as he air boxed or watched the sledgehammer punches land during a match. He had a treasure trove of VHS tapes of boxing matches from the 1960s and 1970s.

"Take your time. Relax." *Jab, jab.* "Yes. Dance. Float. Okay, slow. Watch him. Lean in, but don't jab." *Huuhh, huhh, huuhh.* The boxer just landed punches to the chin and the stomach.

They each prepared in their own way for Dad's final hearing the next day. Mom called in the prayer warriors. Dad watched one of his favorite boxing matches.

The next day, he walked up the never-ending concrete stairs to the courthouse for his case: Verdell Smith versus Globalwest Steel on Second Lake. Even as he walked up these stairs, he was already focused on the next case on his radar and thought how it would feel to climb the stairs of the supreme court, pass by the marble columns, and walk under the inscribed words, "Equal Justice Under Law."

CHAPTER 16
THE WALK OF CONFIDENCE

DAD LEARNED to live with his physical loss and just embodied it in his persona. He wore a prosthetic leg that caused him to limp, so he reset his walk to look like he had a slight pimp. It was the 1970s after all. It was a cool walk, and most people had no clue he was injured. He would then wear fedoras and tilt them to the side. He tried to live a normal life and ignore the pain. He understood how important his walk was to his confidence. You can tell a lot about people by their gait and posture. There is a reason why models spend hundreds of hours perfecting their catwalk. He knew that your confidence level dictates how people treat you, so he chose not to trade in his confidence for his injury.

The injury had to adjust to him and not the other way around. His resilience was remarkable.

Dad was handsome and was the essence of swag, which to me translates into charm, charisma, cool, and intelligence. He was an alpha male, so we can add an *a* at the end for SWAG-A. He held deep conversations on any topic for hours or acted silly and danced around making the crazy faces that children loved and made them fall laughing and giggling hysterically. He loved to laugh, and I have many memories of him having a blast as he watched funny movies and good comedians. I am so glad he found laughter and joy, despite the tragic experiences he had in his life. I stood on his feet, and we would dance. Gabrielle and I would fall asleep on his chest as he reclined in his favorite chair in the living room. He would snore, and we would sometimes lie there and listen to his heartbeat, feeling protected from the world.

We would play the eyebrow raising game, seeing who could raise individual eyebrows one at a time. We would watch *Star Trek* together, which is where my interest in science fiction began.

The trauma he experienced throughout his life was unbelievable. I choose to focus on his love for his children and the good times.

Sometimes we forget our parents had lives before we arrived on the scene. We will never know their trials and tribulations but must remember they are human, and they did the best they could with the hand they were dealt. The older we get and the longer we are on our life's journey, the bigger heroes they become in our lives.

In college, I met many students who had to overcome a physical challenge like my dad and would love to also honor their resilience and perseverance.

In college, I worked for the Students with Disabilities department. I was happy to be in the department. We catered to students with disabilities, including veterans. It was a fantastic job with great experience for a college student.

I began working there right when the Americans with Disabilities Act (ADA) law was about to pass, and it was a frenzy of activity. It was an honor to work in this department as this law was passed, and it was a great achievement. It should have been called the Department of Kindness. All who worked there sincerely cared about these students, and I fit right in.

Everyone was welcomed with a genuine smile and a little small talk when they entered the office. The head of the department, a kind and supersmart Mexican woman who told me to keep smiling, was one of my first mentors. She also pulled me aside one day and corrected my pronunciation of *ask*, not *ax*.

I was an honors English student in high school but yes, I did pronounce *ask* this way. I am writing it here because it is a common mispronunciation that can be easily corrected.

The students came sometimes to hang out because it was a welcome place, and all the employees and directors had a good heart. The new ADA law was big news in the country, and businesses had to adjust. It was a big win for the community. I remember this Puerto Rican veteran who was in a wheelchair. I wish I could find him today. He always had a smile and wanted to make you laugh. He was a regular at the center and stayed in the happy zone.

I had no idea how relevant the ADA law would become in my career. I would later see the execution of the law decades later as a dealmaker in commercial real estate, at times representing the tenant or the landlord. What was disheartening to see was the predatory lawsuits launched on business owners for a quick buck when their businesses weren't up to code, but they were not given adequate time to make changes to their building.

Millions of dollars have been lost by businesses because they weren't given ample time to adjust. I'm glad to see that a law passed that gives businesses the opportunity to make adjustments within a reasonable time frame.

What's interesting is I never thought of my dad as disabled, even when I worked in this department. His body may have been, but his actions and mentality were not. They were whole.

I remember the first time I saw Dad with the blue handicapped car emblem on his rearview mirror, and I wondered what it was doing in his car. I stopped and was perplexed, and it took me a few seconds to register that he did qualify to have the decal. Also, when he parked in handicap parking spaces, I always had to remind myself of his physical challenge.

Now, I understand why disabled people many times will turn down help because they're doing everything they can every day to keep their frame of mind in a position of strength and adaptability. They need to believe they can do it, and they need you to believe too. These are the real overcomers. These are the people who should be traveling the country giving speeches and Ted Talks. Their ability to get out of bed every morning, work, raise kids, and live their lives is commendable. Imagine what their daily conversations are with themselves. What are their mantras, their meditations, affirmations, the biblical scriptures they hold on to? These are conversations of perseverance, hope, belief, power, and a conquer-all attitude. These are the real towers of power.

As I look back, I see a similar confidence that I saw in my dad in many of those students. Someway, somehow, they turned on the *I will survive* switch and forged ahead into their future with peace and joy in their hearts, cherishing every moment of their lives. When you learn to cherish life more, you live it with more intention, gratitude, and vigor.

FAITH

In this section, I discuss one of the hottest topics in the world: What is your guiding light? For me, it is an anointed breeze that pushes and guides me through my day-to-day life. It's a friendship, a never-ending comforter, my biggest cheerleader, a protector, and a place that I call home. In this section, I touch on my faith journey and those who are on it with me.

CHAPTER 17
FRIEND TO YOUR SOUL

After Job had prayed for his friends, the LORD restored his fortunes and gave him twice as much as he had before (Job 42:10 NIV).

BFF, homie, my dude, partnuh, my girl, girlee, best friend, spiritual sister, sister in Christ, we go waaayy back, bud, good buddy, roadie (Dad's favorite), amigo, sister girl…so many ways we describe friends. It usually comes from an emotional place deep inside us that expresses joy, happiness, and appreciation. I believe God puts us together like grapes on a vine.

I woke up and opened an email from Andreanna, a commercial real estate dealmaker whom I met in my industry, with the intro "Monica, I could not sleep, God woke me up to pray for you." This email was sent August 2015, and the prayer touched me so much that I printed and saved it. It was timely then and still carries a blessing today. It is July 2021, and I have come across this prayer email.

This is my girl Andreanna. When we met in 2000 at an industry conference, we instantly became friends, and she immediately began praying for me. I remember the first voice mail prayer I received from her. Yes, you heard me, voice mail prayer. I was in awe that someone would take time out of their busy workday to leave a voice mail. The greatest gift a friend can give you is prayer, which equals love.

I didn't know it at the time, but Andreanna is an intercessor. According to her, an intercessor is a watchman. She said to me, "They sit up very high, and they see things. God reveals things to them because He knows He can trust them. If He puts something on their heart, they will pray."

What I think is so beautiful is that God assigns intercessors to people. Sometimes it's that stranger God instructed to pray for you as they passed you on the street.

Do you realize there may be people in your life interceding for you—praying for you—and you have no idea? Over the years, I've regularly received voice mails from Andreanna with deep, spirit-guided prayers. I disliked changing phones because I had saved her prayer voice mails. Thank God we are still friends, and she is still praying for me. Now she also sends me YouTube videos of sermons and songs that are always perfect timing and the topic I need. I always listen because I know her direction comes from God. Twenty years later, she's still praying for her buddy.

Please take a moment to ask God to bless your intercessor(s), and if you are one, thank you for your obedience, sacrifice, service, and commitment.

It is beautiful when you know God has placed this special soul in your life and you see all the healing, help, and joy they bring. I think back to some of my friends who have been with me through some challenging and joyous times and some for only a short season. I love you, and here's to happy times.

Thank you, Andreanna.

Audra Hagan is also one of my intercessors and a friend for decades.

Audra, Audra, Audra:

Audra, I have watched you conquer everything on your plate with style, grace, and wisdom. You are a mother, wife, executive, and now have the audacity to go for your PhD. Who are you, and where did you come from? No one multitasks like you. Every conversation with you is the perfect amount of laughter, tough love, and fun.

You have been the lighthouse friend in my life. Your light is always on, so I always know where to find you. During my storms, your light seeks me out and pulls me back safely to shore…sometimes crawling.

Usually, the first sentence out of your mouth is the most important. It's heavy with mother wisdom and direction. Your words are so potent, you can almost touch them. You cut to the core of the issue and dig out the roots. No problem is safe in your presence. Your counterattack is lethal, and you shred the attacker without breaking a sweat.

Your voice screams power, even when you whisper. My God, I thank you for sending me such a giant as a friend. But then, you are beautiful and kind with the biggest heart in the world. You and your husband seek out people who need help, sometimes taking in strangers in your home.

We can go months or years without speaking, but the bond is still strong. You always have time for me and my life. The tougher the storm, the tougher and more resilient your response. You never flinch, you win.

I'm not sure when you started, but you were probably my first intercessor outside of family. I had to mention you. Thank you for your continued prayers and friendship. They mean the world to me. There is only one Audra in the world, and I thank God that He sent me one of His elites.

Reader, I asked Audra what an intercessor means to her, and this was her response: "Intercessors are a guard. We are not afraid to go to war in prayer. I am on the lookout for people. You can't play with prayer. According to your faith, so be it."

Thank you, Audra, and may God continue to bless you, your path, and your family.

> *A friend loveth at all times, and a brother is born for adversity* (Proverbs 17:17, KJV).

I wish I could throw a parade for all the intercessors. To my other intercessors, I thank you, and may God continue to bless you.

To sum up intercessors in four words: they live to give.

CHAPTER 18
WALKING THE RED CARPET

For you created my inmost being; you knit me together in my mother's womb. I praise you because I am fearfully and wonderfully made... (Psalm 139: 13–14 NIV).

I AM a daughter of the Most High. I need only prove myself to God, not men. God is my measuring stick... My worth, intelligence, beauty, and status matter only to God. I strive to impress God.

I belong to the Believer group. Freedom is understanding God's unmatched love, unity, and power. His power is exponential. I pray that you experience this immeasurable happiness and be submerged in his glory.

They wouldn't stop. The tears. The tears. The pure tears. I couldn't stop them. Nor did I want to. I tried to casually wipe the first few tears as I approached the small stage. I smiled with every inch of my being. Oh, they were coming stronger now. I had never cried like this before.

The tears were flowing on their own... I felt the Spirit of God was with me.

Three of my friends came to the church in Marietta, Georgia, for my baptism. As I walked out of the auditorium toward the small stage, one of the friends was so happy for me she got a touch of the Holy Spirit and her legs buckled.

I was first in line for the first baptism of 2020 at a church with two pastors. This church nurtured me and welcomed me with open arms upon my arrival. I watched and waited as everyone else got in line behind me, and the pastors completed setup for the baptism.

Barefoot, black leggings, large T-shirt, hair pulled up in a ponytail, and praising God in my heart, I was prepared for rebirth, transformation. I walked down the Red Carpet to Life. The Blood of Jesus was saving me.

My friend took pictures. He is a professional photographer and gave this moment its due—treated it like a celebration.

"Monica, look over here."

He pointed the camera at me and waited for my eyes to lock with the direction of his lens. Smiling, I looked at the camera and waved. The Holy Spirit descended on me, and the tears kept flowing. Some people decided at the last minute to get baptized. It's never too late. That's right. Come on in. The water is "holy." It felt like a baptism party. I loved the openness of it. They jumped in line and changed their lives in an instant. Everyone was happy, excited, and the atmosphere was charged.

The pool was just large enough to sit down in.

"I will pray for you as you enter," Pastor #1 said.

"Okay. Thank you," I said in between tears. I'd waited approximately fifteen minutes for things to start and shed tears the entire time.

I watched as Pastor #2 got in position. There were two more people, one who helped me in the pool and someone who led me out of the pool. People poured out of the auditorium now and gathered around the pool to watch and celebrate the first baptism of the year.

My heart filled with gratitude. It was my second time being baptized.

The first time was as a child in the 1970s. I remember sitting next to Mom at Antioch Baptist Church in E.C. "The doors of the church are open," the Antioch pastor said, and I remember just feeling compelled to get up and walk to the altar.

Amen and sounds of joy came from the audience as they watched me make the biggest and wisest decision of my life. I turned around, stood at the altar, and waited for what was next. A few weeks later, I was in a white robe stepping into a pool behind the pulpit as the elders of the church sang "Take Me to the Water" with a timeless harmony. It was a melodic message to the heavens that another child was joining the family and was a request for God to meet me at the altar.

The elders are royalty. Where did they go? Have they decreased in numbers in today's churches? Let's get them back in the churches across the land. How do some churches function according to the Word without them? There are countless areas in the Bible where elders were depended on for guidance and were part of the foundation and hierarchy of the church. They work in conjunction with the pastor. This was a biblical checks-and-balances system that God put in place. Pastors, leaders, and kings depended on the elders. I distinctly remember the love I received from them—the love they had for Christ and the love they had for their church. Their prayers were powerful—rich with insight, Holy Spirit, and life experiences.

Back to 2020... As an adult, doing it again, I really understood the meaning, having years of mother wisdom and father experience behind me. This is beautiful. I made it. I am back where I belong. Under his wings, taking refuge. Walking into my future with Jesus in my heart and scriptures on my lips. I have the biggest protector and life guide.

> *He will cover you with his feathers, and under his wings you will find refuge; his faithfulness will be your shield and rampart...* (Psalm: 91:4 NIV).

"Step up, please," Pastor #1 said.

I was instructed how to turn around, sit, let them put my head back, raise up while pinching my nose the entire time, stand, turn around, and exit down the stairs into the nearby bathroom. I cried all the way into the water. When I came out, I stopped crying. I was a new creature. The audience clapped loudly and praised God.

My friends screamed my name as my head was gently placed into the water. I slowly exited the pool dripping wet with the beautiful baptism water that was carefully prayed over and entered the bathroom. Yes, it was done.

I dried off, changed, and exited the bathroom with a white T-shirt on that read *Grace*. I could hear the echoes of the singing and dancing in heaven as they celebrated with me, and I joined my friends who were waiting for me. We headed to brunch. My friends treated me, and I took the glow of salvation with me and still carry it today.

A few weeks later, I attended a different church, Greater Community Church of God in Christ (COGIC) in Marietta, Georgia. As soon as I walked in the door, I took a pause to honor the Spirit of God in the walls, the air, the ceiling. Decades of worship and praise in that building...you could feel His presence. This is the Deep South, so this church was a lighthouse during civil rights, a storm shelter for the weary.

My God, was His presence potent in this place. The sermon was incredible, and the choir had you on your feet on the first note... I was at the altar with head back, eyes closed, trying to touch the door of heaven, and then it happened. I went to my church earlier in the day and then went to COGIC, so I was overflowing in the spirit. Almost drunk in the spirit.

I opened my eyes and experienced the most powerful, divine encounter I'd had with God's presence thus far. What I saw, felt, and heard changed me and was just the beginning. It was not until the following year that a prophet/pastor would clarify why I had this experience.

So, when you are at church or in your house and full of the Holy Spirit, stand up, tilt your head back, and sing loudly and boldly to make sure heaven hears you. You leap to higher heights in the spirit when you sing the song out loud and let it fill you. I left that church a new creation and was able to personally tell this to the pastor of COGIC when I had the opportunity to meet him as I left the church that night. What a service! One of my dreams is to one day sing a gospel song with my friend Charlene Stepney. Stay tuned.

CHAPTER 19
IT'S A "LOVELY DAY"

BEFORE I KNEW IT, I was dancing. Hands out, holding Dad's hands. Feet on his feet, and we were dancing. The song was playing, I closed my eyes, and I was eight years old again. I opened my eyes and saw him smiling down at me, and I looked up with the biggest grin I could muster. I had flashed back to our corner home in Indiana in the 1970s. I was giggling uncontrollably as we stepped side to side. Even with the loss of part of his leg, we were dancing.

I was so excited to get this dancing time with Dad, who constantly had the pull of family and work on his life. In this moment, I was his dancing princess.

As I stood in my kitchen as an adult, in 2021, I stayed in the moment and put my head back and smiled and just sung out loud with the song "Lovely Day."

Yes, it is a lovely day. It is a lovely day to be eight years old without a care in the world. It's a lovely day to be doing my favorite hobby in the whole wide world, dancing. It's a lovely day for daddy-daughter time.

I was having so much fun, Dad asked Mom to put the song on and play it again. It had originally come on the radio, but of course, Dad had it in his highly coveted personal collection. I jumped off his feet for a second to gulp down the remainder of my pop (what we called soda). Mom had split a sixteen-ounce pop between four of us kids, and right before the song came on, she had just poured everyone a glass.

This is when this brand of pop came in a bottle, and wow, the taste in glass was distinctly different. I used to handle that four-ounce glass of pop like it was a fine wine.

"Monica," Dad called me as the song played in the background.

Is that "Lovely Day"? I said to myself, stopping in my tracks.

Oh no, I was just about to drink my pop. This was a stressful moment and likely the toughest decision I would have to make all day. I had to decide between finishing the pop Mom gave me or go downstairs and dance with Dad. My eyes darted back and forth to the drink and to the basement door. *Can I call a friend to help me decide?* Okay, dancing all day every day. Dancer for life! I put down the glass of chilled, crispy, bubbling pop ever so gently and ran down the basement stairs.

There was Dad with his arms out, waiting for me with a smile. I gently placed my feet on the top of his, one foot at a time, grabbed his hands, and he began jammin' to the beat.

I was back in my kitchen in an Atlanta suburb in 2021 finding myself stepping side to side as I did when standing on Dad's feet with my eyes closed, head back, hands up, and smiling. I was back. I kept dancing, not wanting to stop the moment. My phone conversation with Pastor Rich Vera that day was so powerful it took me to this childhood moment with Dad.

Pastor Vera is a pastor and a prophet, and we had a long conversation covering my family and my life. Pastor Vera is known the world over and has traveled to sixty-five countries. I was so glad I was able to get some time with him. I was at home and prayed before the call.

"The devil is a liar. Your dad is in heaven," Pastor Vera said. "He's looking over the balcony of heaven and smiling down at you. He is proud of you. He is happy and whole. He is dancing."

My dad had passed some years ago, and I told Pastor Vera that I wasn't sure if Dad was in heaven. When the Holy Spirit told Pastor Vera that Dad was in heaven, I jerked back in my chair. Had I been standing, I would have collapsed. My soul started crying and weeping. The Holy Spirit was comforting me. The more he told me about my father, the more I cried tears of happiness.

"As a little boy, your father prayed to God to save his father, but his father still died," Pastor Vera continued. "When this happened, it created defiance in your father, and this explains why he went through life defiant, but God had mercy on him because he understood why your dad was defiant, and your dad was baptized as a little boy."

He continued to share more information, and I just listened in shock at the detail of the information. It was a turning point in my life.

My father had a big heart, but now I understood from where the defiance as far as spiritually stemmed.

I was raised in church, and I know that knowing God was so important to my mom that I was likely in her arms as an infant being rocked to sleep while she sat in church. I have very early memories of being in church, falling asleep on my mom, my sisters, wherever I could get comfortable. But my spirit was absorbing all this holy goodness. Please take your children to church young. It makes a difference.

I continued to watch Pastor Vera and enjoyed his sermons and teaching, and while watching a live sermon on Facebook, he announced that he would begin personally teaching the children before church, and they would be part of the main service with the adults. He said a child could hear the calling of God as young as five years old. I couldn't agree more. I was seven when I heard the call.

I applaud this. Growing up, the children in my church were not separated from the adults during the main service. Why would you not want your child to see the signs, wonders, healing, Holy Spirit at work, prayer, singing, worship, testimonies, deliverance, praise, and hear the sermon? It's an anointed party, and all are welcome.

Please remember, everyone has their personal relationship with God. Only God knows where they will journey after they leave this earth. May God bless you, your family, the children, and your bloodline.

To this day, I am grateful for the messages God sent me by way of Pastor Vera. Prophets are the mouthpiece of God; they communicate what God tells them to share in that moment.

The conversation was full of minute-by-minute prophecy, wisdom, information, knowledge, and insight, and ended with Pastor Vera in prayer. I was grateful that he was gracious enough to speak personally to people. He is truly excited to pray for people.

To God be the glory.

CHAPTER 20
HOLY EXCITEMENT

WHAT WAS THAT? I asked myself as I left my sunroom.

I had walked in to check on my plants. Sometimes I took a break from work to just step in to say hello to my plants and submerge myself in the view of the trees outside the window. These trees talked to me and were there to support my well-being. My old childhood friends, the pine trees, were also outside my window... I wish I could spend more time outdoors. It would be amazing to be surrounded all day by trees and nature. We were never supposed to be this distant from nature for long periods of time the way some of us are. I'll have to add a contemporary cabin in the woods to my prayer list.

My sunroom has a cathedral-like ceiling with Spanish floor tile. I chose clay pots, which blend well with the tile. These plants, which are in the Dracaena family, called my name when I walked down the aisle of Salt's Nursery to add some life to my home. I had never seen anything like them. This plant is a star—I was struck. My friend who has two green thumbs mentioned she had never seen them before. Even one of the employees had not seen them before.

My friend and I knew it was a gift from God. I had prayed before I went to the store that God would select plants for my home.

To my delight, I found a second one, so now I had a pair. One of them immediately grew, but the other took five months. I was starting to get concerned but stayed patient. The plant was green and breathing, so that was good. At least it had a pulse.

One day, as I was watching TV and turned to get a glance at my plants in the sunroom, I noticed the second plant was growing. I glanced regularly to just say *what's up* telepathically, and sometimes I said hello and good morning out loud and told them how beautiful they were. I leaped out of my seat, went over to the plant with a smile, like a mother about to measure her child's growth on the wall with a ruler.

I touched it and said out loud, "Thank you, Jesus."

It had spent a night outside of the pot when I first got it, so I figured that could have temporarily slowed the growth, but not for five months. I was so proud she was growing. It immediately made me think of life of the last twelve months (being sheltered in place due to the global pandemic that began in 2020) and when you take time to regroup, nurture yourself, or dig your roots deeper to prepare for what's next. So even though you may not think you're making progress, if you're praying, being good to yourself and others, and on your Godly path, you're still growing. You are just digging deeper in the dirt and fortifying your roots—your foundation.

The aloe vera was growing and happy in my sunroom, and the bamboo needed some tender loving care. The plants take my breath away every time I look at them, so I was happy the second plant started to grow.

What is it about the color green? You just can't take your eyes off it. When I look at trees and plants, my eyes drink up the color and digest it into my mind, body, and soul. Just looking at plants and trees gives me life. As I walked out of my sunroom, I thought about the glory of God and the glorious conversation God had with me via Pastor Vera. I felt this overwhelming well of excitement in my belly. I smiled and said, *Thank you, Jesus* and allowed the amazing deep-down-in-your-soul well to wash over me. During our conversation, Pastor Vera told me I would be an evangelist. God spoke to me a few weeks prior, so this was confirmation.

It was a typical morning, and as soon as I woke up, I heard a voice next to me say, "You are going to be a pastor." I know people get their calling in various ways, but I guess God said, "I will have to speak it to her when she first wakes up when she's by herself and not distracted so she is clear it's from me."

Wow. I had no doubt it was from God, and I knew my life had just changed.

Pastor Vera also prophesized that I would have a ministry for the marketplace. Once I received the confirmation from the pastor, I took a few moments to really think about the honor and responsibility of being a pastor. It's an amazing feeling to know I'll build and increase my relationship with God. It's an honor to know this is what God will have me do. I can't wait to get started on this journey.

> *But thou shalt remember the LORD thy God: for it is he that giveth thee power to get wealth, that he may establish his covenant which he sware unto thy fathers, as it is this day* (Deuteronomy 8:18 KJV).

> *And observe what the LORD your God requires: Walk in obedience to him, and keep his decrees and commands, his laws and regulations, as written in the Law of Moses. Do this so that you may prosper in all you do and wherever you go* (1 Kings 2:3 KJV).

CHAPTER 21
HOLY SURGEON

"GOD OPENED a portal for a child tonight. Thank you, Jesus!" Pastor Vera said during a Sunday evening church service.

The audience celebrated in agreement with clapping and amens. At a future service, the mother testified of the miraculous healing her child received that Sunday.

I had arrived for the Sunday evening service at Pastor Vera's church after driving from Atlanta. It was a beautiful Sunday afternoon drive. I hit some traffic, but that was par for the course. It was my first drive from Atlanta to Florida, and I was looking forward to doing it again. So good to get out of town. It was 2021, and I'd been sheltered in place for over a year due to the global pandemic that began in 2020. It was a great reason to take a trip: praise, worship, Word, and healing. The welcome mat had been rolled out, and I couldn't get there soon enough. Moonroof was open, coconut water, green tea, and praise-and-worship songs blasted on the radio. Let's go!

I pulled into the parking lot and could hear the beautiful praise-and-worship music wafting from the building. It is a one-level white building, and parking was available. Yes. After living in Chicago and New York City, I still automatically gave thanks when I saw free and available parking. I stepped out of the car, stretched to the heavens, and felt the blood flow to my legs. I absolutely loved road trips. They were such a peaceful time where you can hear yourself and converse with God.

Years ago, I began turning my phone off at night, turning down the ringer or turning off email notifications. I did this when I got my first cell phone. It was something about it that just immediately felt invasive, like you are having a conversation with someone, and someone just walks in the room, interrupts you, and starts talking. Or if you're praying, watching TV, taking a walk, enjoying watching the paint dry, in a meeting, et cetera, and someone just walks in and starts talking. I've always valued my quiet time, and the cell phone is not too big on etiquette or wait your turn.

Do you realize how much creativity comes when you are quiet and spending time with yourself? I wondered. How can people hear God's voice if they're constantly preoccupied? Now, you're seeing a realization of how important quiet time is and its health benefits by some cell phone users who are beginning to buy flip phones again or better monitor their phone time.

The atmosphere at the church was charged—the Holy Spirit was present. I felt it when I walked in the door. As soon as I walked in, a nice gentleman ran to open the sanctuary door.

As I entered, a lovely spirit, a woman holding guard at the entrance to the sanctuary, said, "Hello and welcome." Smiling, she ushered me to a seat on the end of the aisle.

I did a quick spiritual scan of the room and felt warmth. People smiled at me as soon as I sat down.

The five-person choir was singing, and Pastor Vera joined them. I could tell I was in for a great service.

Reader, have you witnessed the touch of God's love?

"And God is healing your organ right now… Now I see an angel touching your knees… Your knees are healed." Pastor Vera moved from person to person being guided by the Holy Spirit, passing out prophecy, administering healing and deliverance, and translating words of grace and mercy as he met people.

I could see God's tender touch on the pastor. I spoke with him on the phone and then drove down to Orlando to visit his church. It was amazing to watch this holy surgeon, through God's glory, heal people with God's precision and power. On any given Sunday, people witnessed mental, physical, and spiritual healings. It was like seeing God's pure love in the physical.

He told people why they were sick, what they were sick with, and how they would be healed. I don't know if people understand the dedication and sacrifice this gift requires. We only see the healing side at church, but to have this gift requires incredible obedience and responsibility to the Word of God. The straight-and-narrow life that is required alone is an accomplishment, but it's very rewarding.

This church is all about the Word, the whole Word, and nothing but the Word. No other fillers, preservatives, or unnatural flavors. This was refreshing to see and experience.

As I drove out of the parking lot of the church, I said to myself, "I will definitely be back."

Reader, the first time I felt the healing touch of God at a church was a few years back in 2019, and it was amazing. I will try to describe what is a custom-made, individual experience from God. We are all given gifts. Unfortunately, some will leave the earth not knowing what their gifts are or not knowing all of them.

Everyone gets multiple gifts. It's very important you know what they are as they were given to you to help the body of Christ. God just passes out gifts like holy candy. Some people get the gift of healing, evangelizing, prophesizing, singing, dancing, et cetera, but let's be clear, gifts are to be used for the Kingdom of God, and one is to be directed by God when and how to use them.

> *Above all, love each other deeply, because love covers over a multitude of sins. Offer hospitality to one another without grumbling. Each of you should use whatever gift you have received to serve others, as faithful stewards of God's grace in its various forms. If anyone speaks, they should do so as one who speaks the very words of God. If anyone serves, they should do so with the strength God provides, so that in all things God may be praised through Jesus Christ. To him be the glory and the power for ever and ever. Amen* (1 Peter 4:8–11 NIV).

Pastor Vera exhibits gifts of miracle healing, prophesy, deliverance, spiritual discernment, and more. If you haven't experienced the healing power of a healing pastor, please allow me to explain. You see, people fall to the floor because the power of God just puts them there. It could feel electric. You could feel light as a feather or weighed down to the floor. I've had different experiences.

One time, the Holy Spirit took me straight to the floor, and I felt pinned down as the Holy Spirit touched me with its power. Wonderful experience. It is an indescribable feeling. It's truly beautiful. Some people have described feeling heat and seeing light. Others have described out-of-body experiences and being taken to heaven. You feel like pure love just touched you; you float to the floor. I know there's an angel there gently guiding me to the floor. There are also people stationed behind you to catch you, but they're getting help from God. I can feel it.

While you're lying down, you feel the power of God enveloping you. This presence is here to cleanse you, purify you, share information and revelation. You rise a new creature. (*Pastor Vera gave a sermon in January 2023 that discussed the term "New Creature."*) This is why so many people rush to the altar when a called healer, pastor, or prophet is in the house.

So, healing and prophecy are gifts, but there are others. Can you imagine if the healers just kept this gift to themselves? Thank God for the ones who are walking in God's path. Find out what your gifts are and start using them according to God's will, glory, timing, and instruction.

Brothers and sisters, I want you to know about the gifts of the Holy Spirit. You know that at one time you were unbelievers. You were somehow drawn away to worship statues of gods that couldn't even speak. So I want you to know that no one who is speaking with the help of God's Spirit says, "May Jesus be cursed." And without the help of the Holy Spirit no one can say, "Jesus is Lord."

There are different kinds of gifts. But they are all given to believers by the same Spirit. There are different ways to serve. But they all come from the same Lord. There are different ways the Spirit works. But the same God is working in all these ways and in all people.

The Holy Spirit is given to each of us in a special way. That is for the good of all. To some people, the Spirit gives a message of wisdom. To others the same Spirit gives a message of knowledge. To others the same Spirit gives faith. To others that one Spirit gives gifts of healing. To others he gives the power to do miracles. To others he gives the ability to prophesy. To others he gives the ability to tell the spirits apart. To others he gives the ability to speak in different kinds of languages they had not known before. And to still others he gives the ability to explain what was said in those languages. All the gifts are produced by one and the same Spirit. He gives gifts to each person, just as he decides (1 Corinthians 12:1–11 NIrV).

THE DANCE OF LIFE AND COMMERCIAL REAL ESTATE

How do you cope with extreme change and challenges? In this section, I discuss my mechanisms for survival in the unknown. I also crack the door open for a brief look into the mysterious but powerful world of commercial real estate (CRE). Come on in and join the conversation.

CHAPTER 22
YOU DANCE ON 1 OR ON 2?

"YOU DANCE ON1 OR ON2?" Mr. Mambo Suave asked.

This may seem like a simple little question, but which of these seemingly harmless numbers you chose would decide who would ask you to dance and how much fun you would have that night. I am talking about salsa dancing, of course. Or, depending on the style... mambo. Salsa On1 and On2 have two distinct styles and start on a different beat/have a different count.

On2 starts on the second beat and includes a lot of freestyling. I am referring to New York Style Salsa On2, New York Style Mambo On2, or Eddie Torres Style when I mention On2. New York Style Salsa On2 is now the world-favored style, and quite frankly, it was one of the reasons I was excited to move to New York City. If you like salsa dancing, it is nearly impossible to resist the gravitational pull of this style. It is lightning fast, and the transitions are silk on speed. The majority of New York City dances On2, which is danced tight and right —you do not use a lot of floor space. Just like New York City real estate, the dance floor space at these elite dance studio events is highly coveted.

Salsa On1 is flashy, bigger moves, flamboyant with lots of dips. It is more ballroom style and a ton of fun. I dance both styles. Sometimes the terms *salsa* and *mambo* are used interchangeably, but technically, they are different, and salsa evolved from mambo. The origins of mambo dancing and rhythms came from west-central Africa. The drumbeats and music always get me out of my seat, and I adore how some of the lyrics pay respect to women, serenading them with its timeless rhythms.

Back to the dance floor... Mr. Suave, who wore a stretch white button down, three-hundred-dollar jeans, and professional dance shoes, asked again, "Are you On1 or On2?"

I froze. I'd just begun taking On2 lessons, and he'd smelled a newbie as soon as I took the first step. Here goes.

"Wellll, I originally learned in Chicago, so, so, so I learned On1, but I've been taking On2 lessons..." I rambled.

He looked me up and down, paused, looked around to see how many cool kids (the clique of the best On2 dancers in New York City) were watching, grabbed my hand, and we hit the dance floor.

Whew! That was close, I apparently passed the test, I said to myself. He was a well-known dancer in New York City, and if his dance partner was not up to par with his skill level, he would not ask them to dance again. I was glad he took the risk to dance with me, but I don't know what would've been worse, dancing with him or sitting that song out until a guy who did not care what beat I danced on asked me to dance.

I saw his red mambo cape come out as we approached the middle of the dance floor. He pushed up his sleeves, smoothed his long hair back, put on his mambo posture, and glided to the floor.

He looked at me with a *don't mess up 'cause ya know I'm one of the best dancers in this joint, so your On1 better be On2 tonight* expression.

I hid the nervousness, stretched out my toes, aligned my posture in anticipation, and offered him my hands as a humble submission to his lead.

I was now the passenger, being driven by one of the best dancers in the dance studio. Tito Puente, the iconic Latin jazz composer, musician, and band leader, met us on the dance floor, and he was tearing up the room in the dance studio as usual—even the shyest of dancers leaped to their feet when "Ran Kan Kan" came on.

He and I instinctively knew we must bring our A to this game if nothing else but to respect this legendary song. I wore flat black jazz shoes, a freshly done pretty-in-pink manicure, deep pink lipstick, a smidgen of eye liner, fitted blue jean capris, and a burgundy tank top. Clearly, I was ready to sweat.

The year was 2010 or 2011, and I was at the most popular mambo/salsa On2 social in New York City. It just happened to be in a Chelsea dance studio and walking distance from my apartment. People flew to New York City from around the world just to come to this social. DC residents would do a round trip via train in less than twenty-four hours. As we started to dance, a crowd gathered because Mr. Showman had a new victim—*ummm*, that would be me. The best of the best grabbed their willing and unwilling partners and hit the dance floor.

It looked like a scene from *Fame*, and you would think it was choreographed. It was some of the best impromptu mambo dancing in the world. It was fast, unforgiving, and I loved it. I always pinched myself when I walked in. Having danced my whole life, I only dreamed of being in this kind of environment. It was a long way from Indiana.

He spun me ten times in a row, and I stopped on a dime, not even changing my eye blinking pattern. While he turned me, I picked up one foot off the floor and turned 360 degrees on the other foot several times in a row—one of my signature moves. My breathing was moderate but calm. I soaked up the notes and interpreted them with my body.

Mr. Suave started out with amateur dance moves, which I conquered with ease. A true gentleman, I appreciated that. He gauged my dance level before he let loose. Oh, here we go, he was off to the races, and I responded in kind as if I knew what he was going to do before he did it. When a dancer was this good and the music was this fast, it's all instinct. The brain can't respond fast enough to keep up.

He was happy as he scanned the audience for fans, and they came. I melted into his dance steps, not missing a move. I'm a highly sensitive dancer. I can sense the slightest change in my partner's movement, pressure, mood, and direction. As the lead, men are driving the bus and must create dance moves, patterns, and essentially choreograph the dance in real time. As a follow, I have to understand what the lead is instructing me to do and keep up with his choreography with vigor and energy. I've learned to sense what's next by my partner's style, bravado, and attitude.

He looked shocked at me several times because he put down some extremely complicated dance patterns that I gobbled up on the fly. I had entered the mambo-telepathic zone, and he saw it.

One after another, many dancers came to see us dance, so let the show begin. As a teenager, I learned modern dancing, so I mixed modern, salsa, On2 mambo/salsa, and a sprinkle of house music dancing in my style. I just called it my style. I do what I feel. Every time I dance, I am grateful to God for music and the ability he has given me to do it and enjoy it. I left "life" and all its responsibilities, my coat, boots, and the Great Recession's aftershocks at the coat check and entered a world where the best dancers ruled in an imaginary dancers' kingdom with its own hierarchy.

One thing everyone had in common was they loved to dance. You had Puerto Ricans, Jamaicans, Cubanos, Columbians, Nigerians, Mexicans, African Americans, Caucasians, Japanese, South Koreans—visitors from around the world and people from all over the country.

The first rule of salsa dancing is don't ever judge a book by its cover. The nerdiest dude could be the best dancer in the place. Salsa is a level playing field where skill, swag—especially arrogant swag—will get you a dance with *every* woman in the room. We were there to sweat. We were there to celebrate mambo. We were there to celebrate freedom of movement, expression, and the love of dance. It is a community, it is joy, it is living a mambo life. Who cared what you were wearing and what you looked like? All we cared about is *Can you dance On2?*

When the first song ended, I asked Mr. Suave if he wanted to continue, and he said yes and immediately spun me out so I could start the second song in "shine" mode. This was a great way to start the song. I started with slow-to-fast shoulder rolls and did three solo turns in a row. This told me that I passed the test. He didn't run off the dance floor after the first song. The second song was Afro Latin jazz, and I pulled out my knife and fork. We had now downloaded each other's style and could dance with each other with our eyes closed. This was the beauty when you're an advanced dancer and you mesh with a great partner. He pulled out more tricks and joined me in freestyling.

I reciprocated and tried not to smile. As you know, reader, this is hard for me. It would be totally un–New York cool to have smiled at that moment, so I just smiled inside.

Wow. Mr. Mambo Suave is so good he made my sweat dance. He dipped me as the song ended. We grabbed each other's hands, said thank you, and walked off the dance floor.

I headed to the bathroom, dried off, and headed toward the coat check, where life—the real world—was awaiting my return.

As I walked to my apartment, I flashed back to my corner home in Indiana where my love of dance began.

"Monica, Moonniicccaaaa," Dad called to me.

I was in the middle of a dream. My uncle Kenneth had just handed me an ice cream sandwich. I was reaching for it with all my might, and I heard my name being called.

I rolled out of bed, put on shorts and a white-and-red striped T-shirt.

"Where are my house slippers?" I said to myself.

Mom would've been upset if I walked downstairs with no shoes on. Plus, the floor was cold. I heard the muffled music as I got ready. I was still half asleep, but it was calling my name.

"Moooonniccccaaa," Dad said again.

It was just loud enough to wake me, but in a tone that wasn't startling. I knew the difference between an angry dad beckoning and an inviting one. I started automatically shaking my five-year-old head to the beat of the music coming from the basement. I looked under the bed for my other green fluffy house shoe.

"There it is."

I grabbed it and put both on my feet. I didn't want to turn on the light and wake Gabrielle. There was just enough light from the streetlight for me to throw on some clothes. I slowly walked out of my room, through the railway bathroom, and stopped at the top of the basement stairs. I needed to wake up completely before I took on those stairs. There were a lot of them, and I was only five. I could dance, but I still needed some time to carefully walk down steep stairs. Dad called me a third time.

"I'm coming," I said, still half sleep.

The crowd cheered when they heard my voice—or at least that's what it felt like. It sounded like there were about five people. I distinctly heard a few voices I recognized—a few family members and road dogs or roadies, as Daddy called them. Mom was probably sitting on the leopard love seat sipping on a pop.

I hoped they had their checkbook ready because they were about to get a show. You could get me out of bed at one in the morning to dance, but not for school. Go figure. I was enjoying my ice cream dream, but dance beat out ice cream two to one every day of the week.

I still remember Mom's friend Shirley's face when I danced. I looked at her most of the time. She always lit up when she saw me and never stopped grinning. As a five-year-old, this was like a moth to a light. She sat on the edge of the brown leatherish sofa. As I started to feel the groove of "Get the Funk Out Ma Face," I suddenly went into overdrive doing the rock dance style that was popular at the time (mid-1970s) and rocked my body from side to side as I bent my knees and lowered myself to the ground.

Shirley nearly lost it and laughed. I gave dancing my all, whether two in the afternoon or midnight on a school night. Even then, I had a deep respect for music and the art of dance. Oh, wait a minute. Now I started doing the bump. Here we go, here we go.

So even at a young age, I knew how to get the party started. I see these same traits in me today. Countless times, I am the first to the dance floor or the first to speak up in a meeting or keep the meeting going and the commercial real estate deal alive. Let your children be free and encourage their happiness because this produces children who will soar and seek the things that make them smile.

"Verdell, you are something else," Mom said as Dad got up and started dancing.

I looked over and immediately stopped doing the rock because he was doing the move that got me every time. I mean, this move made us all fall out on the floor in uncontrollable laughter. It was his silly Daddy meets Kermit the Frog facial expression. Even though Dad had his physical limitations, he would dance to make us laugh.

I sat next to Shirley and watched Dad.

He didn't do this dance often, and I wanted to enjoy every minute. Dad was in his black slacks and a white short-sleeved T-shirt.

Dad put his left hand over his chest and stuck the other one straight out toward the wall. He screwed his mouth up like Kermit, pushing his lips in opposite directions, and then started to turn in a circle. He continued to turn.

I appreciated the show. This was his way of saying thank you since I'd come downstairs, so in return, he made me laugh only the way Daddy knew how. He kept turning, then he stopped and scrunched his mouth again and tilted his head. By this time, I fell to the side on the couch with laughter. I could not speak. I ran to Dad, jumped on his feet, and we started to dance. I was having the time of my life.

Yup. I learned early on that people enjoyed watching me dance, but more importantly I'd found something that made me feel like nothing else did. When I danced, I felt electric, empowered, and blissful. Nothing else took me to this place. It was like inhaling joy. So, I threw myself into dance and let it take me to its secret places.

The power of dance has no limits. When you see a dancer move, you are just focused on their body, but the feeling a dancer gets is so much bigger. When we jump or leap, we feel like we are leaping thirty feet in the air. The real movements that we see and feel ourselves doing are supernatural to us. When I twirl, I am gathering all the beautiful and peaceful energy around me and using this momentum to spin. Gravity is a dancer's friend…rhythm, space, time, air, feelings, and emotions. We use them all interchangeably. While I dance, I have a conversation with the music. I translate the meaning of the song into the physical. The music and I are partners dancing down a road of serenity and universal love.

So, this is why I have combined dance in the same section as commercial real estate in this book. Three reasons actually: 1) Commercial real estate is a dance of sorts. A deal can start off as a tango and end in a beautiful waltz; 2) Life is a dance. Where you are in your life depends on the type of music you choose to play and the type of dance you are doing; and 3) I used dance as a temporary getaway or retreat from the demands of commercial real estate and the Great Recession. It also has great health benefits. It is advised that one has a mental and physical retreat to survive in the tumultuous sea of commercial real estate negotiations.

As I finished my walk home from the Chelsea dance studio and entered my apartment building, I waved at the attendant at the granite counter. I finished reminiscing about my earliest dance childhood memories and thought about my mom, who told me to keep dancing.

I know Mom was saying, "Go, Monica, go!" in heaven as she watched me dance. She had passed on some years earlier and loved to watch me dance. But too bad, they were playing a cha-cha as I left. I love cha-cha. Well, there will always be a next time, and so I just cha-cha'd into my apartment while the mambo rhythms floated above my head, eased my muscles with a hot bath, and prepared for a good night's sleep.

XOXOX to you, Mommie.

Recently, I've added liturgical dance to my repertoire and absolutely love it. *When God calls, make sure you answer the phone.*

CHAPTER 23
PINK IS THE NEW RED

VIEW of the Great Recession from my New York City apartment window.

Six on a Thursday morning, I slid out of bed and said my good mornings and thanked God for another day... I thanked and high-fived Jesus. I began my usual self-pep talk to get myself ready for another day of fencing with some of the best negotiators in the business: New Yorkers who brought their A game on a daily, but now they were bringing their A-to-Z game, and I needed to get a good night's sleep to make sure I was ready for the daily deal wrestle.

It was 2009, and five-star sleep could be an unattainable luxury in Manhattan due to the street noise talking to you all night and the city's smorgasbord of food, fun, and culture that always attempted to lure you into their grip 24/7.

Landlords wanted our money, and we didn't want to give them as much money as they wanted, albeit a basic deal wrestle to the bottom line. I worked for a tenant/retailer at the time, and the entire retail real estate/shopping center industry was on high alert trying to negotiate the best deals they could to keep stockholders happy, save jobs, and save profits. My negotiations were with landlords and owners of street locations and shopping centers.

My third-floor apartment at a white-glove building near the United Nations had proven to be a shelter from the outside honks, music, and occasional vocal cabdriver—after I put up two layers of black-out shades, of course. I would have never survived without these black-out/noise-reduction curtains that meant more to me than finding a cab at 3:00 a.m. on New Year's Eve in the Meatpacking District.

It was large for typical Manhattan standards—a full one-bedroom and a living room big enough for a full-size sofa, forever all-time favorite (in apartment buildings in New York City) parquet floors, a breakfast nook/bar, and a full-size bathtub.

I've been in the shopping center real estate/commercial real estate industry since college. Think secret society meets big expense accounts meets multimillion-dollar deals meets partying meets billion-dollar portfolios meets big capital.

Many know not of its existence except those who are in it. People would never expect what went into that Gap store they just purchased a button-down, flip-flops, blue jean jacket, and long-sleeved T-shirt from. It's fast, competitive, and unforgiving. As a Black woman, it's like unknowingly walking into a minefield. I would use all Dad's lessons and talks to endure this take-no-prisoners fight for what is essentially land when it comes down to it. And we know all too well what world history tells us about man's drive to occupy land, and the shopping center industry is no different. (The battle over land is the most common cause for war in history.) Maneuvering in this sea of money, property values, public companies, and ego parades takes a thick skin and a set of unique skills specific to this industry.

I never thought I would have a career such as this, but it certainly came at a price. It's almost unaffordable. Women/minorities have to take out a high-interest loan with a balloon to afford it, which is a big no-no.

So, I was out of bed and headed to the kitchen to soak my greens for my daily juice. I put on a pot of water for green tea and grabbed the newspaper outside my apartment door. As I closed my door and glanced at the front-page story of the newspaper, my phone rang.

"Sister, you up?" Gabrielle asked.

"Yeah. I'm on Eastern time, remember?"

"Oh yeah, that's right. I know you're getting ready for work, I just wanted to make sure we keep in touch regularly. There were more major company layoffs announced yesterday."

"Oh no. Well, hopefully, many of these companies will bring back a lot of these workers, and I pray everyone will land on their feet," I said as I pulled out additional ingredients for my green morning smoothie.

"Let's pray for a minute," Gabrielle requested.

"Okay. You want to lead?"

My sister began to pray for our family, our careers, and the country. This is what you do when there is a problem. Why complain about it when you can pray about it?

The biggest real estate bankruptcy was unfolding. Baby boomers who had ninety-five percent of their savings in the market because that was their marching orders were losing everything. Antidepressant (and other substances) usage was at an all-time high. Marriages were called off; relationships were under attack due to stress and people losing their jobs. Couples held off starting or expanding their families due to a lack of income or concern about the future. Wall Street dudes fled to eastern Europe. I remember reading about two Wall Street friends who became paramedics.

The commercial (retail) real estate industry was pure carnage. People were leaving my industry in droves. It was death all around, and the stench was sickening as there was nowhere to put the dead bodies. (I was going to delete this due to events from 2020 to 2022 but decided to keep it in. I wrote this in 2016 pre-coronavirus. May God bless and keep everyone safe.) They were terrible, terrible, terrible times.

People in my industry for years went to work every day not knowing if they were getting a pink slip. Unfortunately, the cuts weren't fair all the time and not always based on what was best for the company or the person's production. Top dealmakers were let go for frivolous reasons.

If your boss didn't like you, it was an easy ticket for many companies to just purge. Maybe your work was outstanding, but they had someone else they liked more. Pink slip. Maybe they wanted to hire their friend. Pink slip. Maybe a contact called in a "favor." Pink slip. Maybe you got sick due to the increased work overload and stress due to the Great Recession. Pink-slipped and true story a hundred times over. Pink slips were flowing through the streets of New York City due to all the red on Wall Street and companies' bottom lines. This thing went on for an eternity and had the country in a pit bull vise grip. But some chose to quit in order to save their sanity and free themselves of the global economic pressure that everyone was under from the C-suite to the assembly line.

I remember speaking to a landlord dealmaker on the phone. We were negotiating a deal, and it was the first time we'd spoken.

"Hi, Phil. This is Monica from XYZ Company. I'm calling to discuss a deal at your ABC shopping center. You have a minute to discuss?"

"Hi, Monica. Thanks for calling..." He trailed off, and then there was an awkward pause.

"Is that what I think it is? Whoa. It is." I heard tears, and not just tears but the slow-rising momentum of uncontrollable sobbing.

"Hey. Is everything okay?" I whispered so my coworkers couldn't hear the conversation. It sounded like this was about to go confidential.

"I just resigned today," he murmured.

"What?" I said in shock.

And he went on to tell me his story, how stressed out he had been while he sobbed in between words. "I don't care if me, my daughter, and my wife have to live in a shack, I'm getting out of here!"

He went on to say people couldn't believe he would leave during a recession, but he just couldn't take it anymore. He said it wasn't worth it.

"I completely understand, and I agree with you. Save yourself and your family. Real estate is at the center of this calamity, and people have cut back on their shopping. Companies are trying to make their numbers, and it's mission impossible right now," I said in a supportive voice.

"I've been in this industry a while and have seen a lot. I'm resilient and an exceptional dealmaker, but this Great Recession and how it's turning companies into a pressure cooker is just out-of-this-world crazy. I gotta get out while I still can. It isn't worth my life. I would like to see my daughter grow up."

We really didn't discuss the deal. Even though I didn't know him, I provided verbal support of his decision. It was brave but necessary. I wished him the best; we ended the call, and I walked across the street to grab an early lunch and think about the conversation I had just had.

The pain, suffering, and uncertainty that upper management endured had been passed down like secondhand clothes to their employees. I can't imagine how many sleepless nights corporate executives experienced during this period in history. Not to mention public companies. They had shareholders to report to, and their decisions determined who made it to the other side of the mountain alive.

Corporate abuse was on the rise. Employees got cursed out and treated as subhuman.

Those were dark days. I was a commercial real estate broker before the Great Recession began, and Clarissa, a friend in California, in March 2007 warned that it was time to get back in the corporate game again. She shared a conversation she had with Burt, a retailer who owned a few companies.

Reader, I've created a story so you can better understand this conversation. I've negotiated hundreds of commercial real estate deals and am well versed in how these conversations unfold.

"Burt, oh, we were so close to getting your deal done, but my executive real estate committee didn't approve the numbers," Clarissa said. She slowly continued, feeling the bad news register through the phone since Burt did not comment. "…I even had my boss visit two of your stores—"

"I've increased my rent offer three times, and my CFO has put the brakes on any additional increases. We would like to make some semblance of a return if that is okay with your executive real estate committee," Burt quipped in a sarcastic tone.

"My committee just doesn't understand why you won't come up to our numbers. You have fifty-eight locations, and they're all generating north of three million dollars. We're also providing six months of free rent. Well, I guess we aren't making a deal today because we'd like to make a wee bit of money ourselves, you know," Clarissa finished.

"Well, let's keep in touch. Quite frankly, this is disappointing because we spent seventeen months on this deal, not to mention I hired an architect, and—"

"And I told you not to do that. It was too soon. The deal wasn't approved. It's an A-plus center, so you know you have to pay to play," Clarissa continued.

"Maybe it's for the best because my real estate gut tells me it's time to pull back," Burt said, thinking out loud. "I've already sold my stock."

"What do you mean? Are you even fifty yet? You think your all-knowing gut is telling you to sell right now?" She turned around in her chair at work to look out the window and faced the California mountains.

Burt gave a very ominous laugh and said, "I see the signs. My hourly employees who are living paycheck to paycheck are coming to work in luxury cars. I couldn't understand how they could afford it, so I casually did some investigating. I found out they're refinancing their homes and cashing in inflated equity. Some are buying homes out of their price range. The only reason I was going to do this deal with you is your market is millionaires and billionaires, and they're my top customers. Many of them will weather the inevitable economic downturn that's brewing.

"In six months, you'll be begging for my deal, but out of principle and my well-earned ego, I'll graciously decline."

"Wow…okay. Well, good luck in the continued success of your business, and I hope you're wrong, but your theory does make sense. I've noticed a few cracks in the economy's armor myself."

After they said their goodbyes and hung up their phones, Clarissa pulled a notable chunk of her money out of the market and then called me immediately to share her conversation and advise me to go back to a nine-to-five job.

Shortly thereafter, we watched the industry implode. I was back in corporate about six months later, and she worked for a major corporation that was doing what it could to adjust to what felt like a minute-by-minute change of our industry and the world.

I consumed the *Wall Street Journal* every morning as I took the train to work and tried to piece together the path the economy was taking. I lived on the same street where Bear Sterns, a New York–based global investment bank, was located, and literally anyone who walked into their Midtown building seemed like they were sleepwalking. I couldn't even look at it after a while, so I walked on the other side of the street. It was horrible to watch a giant fall and witness the impact on a nation.

My social life changed too. I limited the fancy dinners, danced a lot of mambo, and sang a ton of karaoke at the time to make it through. I had a low or no tolerance to alcohol and other substances, not to mention Dad's tactics to keep me from smoking set a precedent, so I had to find another fix—vice…an outlet. I went to private karaoke rooms and ate snacks and overdosed on cranberry juice. I belted out Anita Baker, Bon Jovi, Lauryn Hill, and Alicia Keys.

One time, someone in the karaoke private room next to me came into my room and high-fived me for my singing. It was such a relief. I really wanted to get deep in the diaphragm to relieve the stress hiding in there. I loved the songs I could just belt out. I felt cleansed and ready to fight another day. I went to sing karaoke weekly, supplementing my workouts. Everyone told me to meditate, but I was too type A for that.

I got a singing coach who was from eastern Europe. She traveled and sang in five different languages. She told me I had three octaves, and my high soprano was pitch perfect and gave her goose bumps. I just thought, *Okay, that sounds cool* and kept getting my relief at karaoke. It was fun. While she was my instructor, I saw her win at the Apollo. She was a jazz singer who played the bass and was super talented.

During the Great Recession, work had intensified for everyone. One day at work felt like you had worked a week. The Great Recession just kept going. One of the most said words at the time was *headwinds*. It was in every newspaper, constantly on the news, and said in every boardroom across America.

I heard *headwinds* or *turning the ship* so many times I was ready to get my captain's license. So here is another nautical analogy of the Great Recession that I think is a pretty good description of this time in history.

The economy was in a one-man skiff in the middle of a hurricane in the Atlantic Ocean in November during a full moon, ninety-degree weather, with an occupant who had just had a steak dinner and chocolate cake for dessert, had a bit too much to drink, was out of drinking water, couldn't swim, no life jacket, no paddles, no flares, no radio. The economy had to die before it could be rebuilt. There was just no way around it. RIP, pre-economy 2007.

The walk light flashed, and the three of us walked across 23rd Street headed toward Madison Square Park in New York City in 2009.

"Do you see what they're doing? Hiring trends?" Jamie, a friend in the shopping center/commercial real estate industry, asked, but she already knew the answer.

"Yes, I see it. I'm not so sure this is the right strategy," I said in a deeply concerned tone as I took the lead and walked toward our destination in the park. The outdoor restaurant was set up in a large kiosk with outdoor seating. It was the perfect day for food, conversation, and talkin' shop. We jumped in the long line that wound toward the order window and continued our industry chat.

Helen looked at the menu and said, "Of course it's not. Everyone knows it."

"Are they sure they should be letting go of the veterans of the shopping center [real estate] industry? The industry vets have been through a few recessions already, not to mention they have redevelopment experience. These malls will be like Humpty Dumpty when this is over. You'll need to put them back together again," I asserted.

Helen and Jamie were in New York for the weekend. I had met Helen ten years before. She was a shopping center executive on the landlord side. She and Jamie were besties and came to New York City yearly to shop and canvass retail stores and retail trends.

They hit up Fifth Avenue, and we were grabbing a bite in Madison Square Park before heading to my favorite hat shop, which had a location near the Flat Iron District.

"I really love this neighborhood. Would love to live down here one day," I said. "I just don't get it." I did a full 360-degree twirl in the park, looking at the pedestrians, buildings, and the buzz of activity around the park.

"They may save thirty or forty thousand dollars in annual salary, but a seasoned dealmaker can make that up in one deal. This recession will require more seasoning. I mean, we are talking five-plus years before we get out of this thing. You need connected, skillful dealmakers to successfully dig our industry out of the canyon this recession will create. The bottom line is chasing its tale at many of these companies," I said as I stood in line in front of Helen.

"What happened to looking at deal sheets, experience, connections, sweat, retail historical knowledge, et cetera?" Jamie asked.

"It's a short-term plan for what could likely drag out for seven years," I commented.

"You'll have to look at these centers with a fresh set of eyes as if they're coming out of the ground. You need to do this as you lease for the future," Helen said as she grabbed her burger from the pickup line. "Redevelopment or new development experience will be a secret weapon for those who have it, even in leasing an existing center."

"I completely agree, Helen. The redevelopment or new development experience gives you an entirely new perspective in leasing a mall. It becomes innate. You really understand what makes a center tick—it's DNA," I said.

Jamie made a dash for the last available table near the water fountain, five feet away from the pickup window, and said, "...really think the industry will suffer for this decision. I agree, they should double down on existing talent with ten-plus years. These people give them the best chance to leap successfully out of the Great Recession.

"The only deals that will be made for the next few years will be favors, and you need contacts to call in a favor and to have *hopefully* previously done a deal with that favor. And let's hope you did a big favor for the retailer on the other end of the phone. As we know in this business, you're only as good as your best contacts. So, all will see how this plays out over the next several years," Jamie finished.

I grabbed a few napkins, sat at the table with my food, and said, "I have concern for the next downturn. If you get rid of the talent today, who trains the new talent and how can the new talent be ready for the next downturn?"

Jamie took three successive gulps of her shake and said, "All good points. Let's continue to pray for each other and that this recession becomes a distant memory. Wow. This shake has me shook! We need to stop by here again before we leave."

"Welll…that is why *Shake* is in the name. It should be called *Shook* because the shake and burger are from a dimension of their own," I said.

"So far, my job seems secure… I guess. We have very little debt and decided early on to work with retailers. We just want to keep the lights on," Jamie said as she finished the shake and reached for the burger.

"That's good to hear. How many deals did you get in this year?" I asked.

"Well, I should make my goal, but I'm not too worried, as I had a stellar year last year and—"

"Last year is last year's news. You have to perform this year to stay on top, my dear," Helen interrupted, "but I know you know this."

"It's so important to manage the stress and not let it manage you," Jamie said, looking off into the distance. "This economy threw everyone for a loop. Hold on, everybody. Hold on."

"God didn't want us working this hard for material satisfaction or to make a living. You can't take any of it with you. You can make incredible money in this industry, but there is a trade-off," Helen said.

"I'm turning in some of the hardest deal packages of my career," I admitted.

"You mean besides the D centers you had to cut your teeth on?" Helen asked as she savored the last bite of her burger.

Reader, shopping centers were ranked A, B, C, and D, and the meaning was literal. The ranking was based on factors including sales per square foot and types of tenants.

I laughed and said, "Oh…you mean the initiation or hazing centers? Oh yeah, God showed up and worked some miracles on those, but I wouldn't want to go back to those days."

STEEL VICTORIES   153

Jamie chimed in, "Whew. It's not so bad when you get the challenging shopping centers [high vacancy rate, declining sales, et cetera] when you're new because you don't know just how much prayer, blood, sweat, tears, and miracles you're going to need. It's when you get them later in your career and you are 'woke' is when they can really sting."

Helen looked through her designer crossover bag for a mirror, touched up her gloss, and said, "Yes, when you get the D centers later in your career, you are thinking, one, this is a setup and I should be looking for another job; two, they think I'm really fantastic and can part the Red Sea—or in this case tear down barricades—or three, they think my contact list is better than what it is."

"You speaketh truth, my sister, but what I mean is I created a way to project recession sales on the deals I'm turning in. We have to be realistic. It's new economic territory, and I must manage expectations. The atmosphere in executive committee didn't feel very kumbaya. It's just strange. There are no CPI [Consumer Price Index] increases. What the what? This is a career first for me. How do we even do our jobs? I don't want to put my name on a deal when I know jobs are disappearing and the trend is looking over its shoulder."

"It's strange times, and numbers don't lie," Jamie said, sitting back in her seat, allowing her body to digest the delicious meal she'd just had.

"I keep checking sales again and again and again, like they're going to reverse course," I said as we threw our meal trash away and headed out of the park.

We bounced around and shopped, stopped for tea, and enjoyed the fleeting time we had with one another. I bid them farewell in the West Village as we visited one of their favorite pizza places for one last slice, and they jumped in a cab and headed to LaGuardia.

A few years passed, and the next time I saw Helen and Jamie for one of their annual trips to New York City was for lunch as I wrapped up a retail deal in The Hamptons.

Helen put her umbrella at the door and walked over to the table and sat down and said, "Wow. The pace of this city is off the charts."

Jamie nodded in agreement. "As soon as your plane lands, you're thrust into this alternate world that is moving at warp speed."

"Yeah. It's like going from ten miles an hour to two hundred miles an hour in an instant. I've traveled all over, and NYC has its own type of intensity. I'm wrapping up a deal here, and I really enjoy the ride out to The Hamptons and getting away from the constant buzz. It really is Planet NYC," I said.

"It's a few years later, and the economy has not fully recovered from the Great Recession and its aftermath," Helen said. "What have we learned over the last few years, ladies? Let's talk career strategy and deal strategy. Things are shifting more than anticipated. Monica, what's the word on the street here in NYC? We know a lot of things happen here first before the rest of the country."

We spent four hours at lunch sharing information from Wall Street to Europe to China. It turned into a true brainstorming session. We didn't leave until each person laid out their work and personal life plan for the next three years and everyone had an opportunity to vet it. This is one of the secrets to staying alive in this business: surrounding yourself with genuine genius.

CHAPTER 24
THE FIGHT WILL FIND YOU; PUT UP YOUR DUKES

YOU ALWAYS HAD to be on guard in the house because Dad was always planning regular sneak attacks. Countless times—too many to remember—Dad would come at me boxing, throwing two-combination punches and an upper cut in a timeline of a millisecond. Yes, this is what I lived with. I knew Dad was an ex-boxer, so he reveled in throwing a punch anytime he could. It was a part of my forced boot camp. I'd be half asleep, grouchy, hungry, not too excited to go to school, and he would appear out of nowhere, even with the prosthetic limb. He would come so close to my face with his punches I could feel the wind. I would scrunch up my face, squeeze my eyes shut, and brace for impact. I am happy he never miscalculated because he was that close.

It was part of the Butch "life is not easy" training. He didn't raise me with kid gloves but treated me as the world would treat me so I wouldn't be shocked or duped by what waited outside the perimeter of our tranquil corner lot.

He wouldn't stop throwing combinations and going full Bruce Lee, the greatest martial arts icon, on you—verbal boxing grunts and noises and all—until you put up your dukes. Then, once he got you to understand you needed to guard yourself, he did not stop until you punched back—and it better be convincing. Then the next level was you had to talk smack and bob and weave. Once you put your guard up, bobbed, weaved, engaged in trading punches, and began talking smack for a minute or two, he would retreat and resume his day. His goal was to remove the discomfort or fear of someone getting in your face and physical contact. He also knew that most attacks are surprise ones, so I had to be able to think and react fast.

It taught me to talk confidently, even when I was fearful, to think clearly and strategically, and manage fear rather than being consumed by it. To this day, I remain calm in crazy situations. It also made me realize that talking smack could get you out of a situation that appeared to have no comfortable or livable exit. He taught me that fighting is both physical and psychological.

I watched him throw punches and bob and weave in the full-length mirror in the basement. He regularly reminisced of his boxing days and jumped in the ring with an imaginary opponent. Even with his prosthetic leg, it was pure skill. His gaze would change to a killing machine, and his imaginary opponent was about to see his shoes up close because he always went for the knockout. He would add in some footwork—what boxers did to trick or intimidate their opponents. It was also done to allow a gap in the fight to study their opponents' moves and emotional state and to line up the perfect geometric angle for their impeding attack. His punches were full of power and precision. He would do this in every mirror that would have him in the house.

After his father died when Dad was a little boy, life at home went in the wrong direction. He was tied to a radiator and beaten when he returned home from school every day. Hard to believe someone could endure that daily. That household needed healing. Thank God his aunt eventually took him in and raised him for a portion of his childhood.

He also was smaller framed and got chased home from school daily by white kids. He started fighting back at school and was just a beast on two feet.

The above events likely contributed to why he was such a lethal boxer. Boxing likely became an outlet for what he experienced at home. His home life could also be why he never celebrated holidays or birthdays because he had more negative than positive childhood memories. He would get angry if we bought him birthday or holiday presents. Sometimes we would rebel and buy them anyway. I'm sure he appreciated them.

When he launched his sneak boxing attacks with air punches, I thought, *This is crazy. I'm a girl. He shouldn't be throwing punches at a girl.* Well, he obviously knew something I didn't—that I would be assaulted while working one day. I think he figured girls get in fights, too, so I had to be prepared.

He fought his way through life and wanted to teach me to do the same. There were no pity parties or "oops, you have a boo-boo" from my father. He understood his assignment as a father, and that was to protect me at all costs. Part of protecting a child is to teach them how to protect themselves. How to never be surprised. How to always be ready so you don't have to get ready. His teachings also included ways to avoid tragedy to begin with. If he were alive today, the first words out of my mouth would be *Thank you.*

CHAPTER 25
MATRIX IN PRADA

NOT MANY PEOPLE know about this occurrence, so I only bring it up to prove that my father did indeed know my future.

I have a petite frame and I wore a new pair of beautiful princess golden Prada sandals with a kitten heel. It was 2004, and I was at one of my industry's large conventions, I had a lighthearted, professional business exchange of words with a male colleague. I thought it was just two people having a witty back-and-forth like I had done countless times in my typical course of conversing with someone.

Next thing I knew, a fist was coming from Canada to hit me. This guy just tried to knock me out! I immediately wielded back like in the Matrix (or Ciara) to avoid being punched in the face, lurched back up and put up my dukes talking smack like my daddy taught me. This defused the situation, and we went our separate ways. The man who tried to hit me was confused by my immediate response. It was then I understood why my father simulated boxing with me. I was appalled by this behavior, but because of Butch's boot camp, I was surprised but not shocked. I would move on to my next meeting and eventually move on to the evening festivities, which included co-hosting the Diversity Reception at the convention.

The purpose of the event was to promote inclusiveness and diversity. As I spoke to the crowd, I couldn't help but think how ironic it was that I was just assaulted, and this event was very much needed so that women and minorities felt comfortable in knowing they would be treated with dignity. When I asked my employer to support me at the event, they did not hesitate, and the president of my company agreed to give a speech. (My white boss and some of my white male coworkers came and supported the event. Thank you!) I witnessed people interviewing, making deals, and wheeling and dealing as the event evolved over the years. It was amazing to be a part of it, and I could now check the "community contribution" box on my life bucket list. This event single-handedly helped elevate African Americans and others in the industry. Contacts are the lifeblood of my industry!

It now offers scholarships, which was one of my primary expressed visions of the group. I remember running around for years networking, entertaining, and gaining valuable contacts before social media had hit its stride. It all came in handy for this event.

All were welcome to this event. A white male commended me while I was interviewing for a job. He knew it was needed. Some people love to see people striving to improve lives for others.

It was great to be the original founder of a diversity movement in the industry and a part of this historical and first-of-its-kind event that continues to this day. Thousands of connections have been made between people from across the country and the globe. I remember connecting a developer building a mall in Asia with a United States developer. The event was working!

I first had the idea to get African Americans and minorities together after attending the large convention in the late 1990s. It went from meeting at restaurants/bars around Vegas (all were welcome) in the late 1990s, to hotel suites in Vegas, and then finally to a banquet hall in Vegas. Harriett Edwards, an industry icon, was right there with me.

In 2004, I received two calls within days of each other from two people who heard I had put together minority events in Vegas, and they wanted to join forces. I said yes, so now there were four of us. We grew the event attendance exponentially, and that is the first year the event moved to a hotel suite. The convention was weeks away, and everything was booked. I scrambled to find a suite and pulled out all the charm. The negotiation skills came in handy... I found a suite. It was a miracle. We had pulled it off in record time. As the president of my company spoke, the room was packed with people nibbling on hors d'oeuvres and appreciating seeing an event like this come to fruition.

People knew I had put together events in the past, and I got word out as quickly as I could, along with the other founders. At the next one, Harriett convinced top-notch speakers, including one of the first Black shopping center major dealmakers, to take the mic at the podium. She also convinced a highly regarded C-suite white female who was a staunch advocate for women in the industry to speak.

It was also Harriett's idea to add the word *inclusive* to the tagline for the event.

Harriett made one of the highest sacrifices any commercial real estate dealmaker could give...her contacts and iconic industry influence. It was a real estate dealmaker convention, so she and I contributed our cherished dealmaker contacts. I moved in the same spirit as I did with the gathering in its infant stage with determination, vision, togetherness, power, and a successful mindset. I like to look back at the beginning and think how one idea can turn into a movement. That's why no idea is too small or insignificant. *Is the tree more important than the seed?* God watered our seed and blessed it. The first time we had the event at the hotel suite, I said, "This is history." It started small, but most things do.

In the early days, we really needed each other. I look at the people who attended the smaller gatherings. (Hi, if you are reading this book. ☺) They are in the industry doing exceptionally well and industry leaders in their own right. What an honor to have met them back then and watch their careers soar.

Reader, I hope you'll take a moment to get to know Harriett Edwards. Harriett has done so much for so many people and doesn't expect the limelight or accolades, so I had to make sure I highlighted one of her many contributions in our industry. Her stories and contributions to the shopping center industry are beyond astounding. She is worthy of a *New York Times* bestselling book.

And applause is in order for all the founders, co-hosts, sponsors, and those who contributed to its success. It took a village!

Diversity Reception photo of Monica speaking (photo credit R. Strimling)

I was so glad the event was a success. At the end of the evening as I prepared to leave and head to dinner, I took comfort in my dad's intense teachings. They had worked. He'd made his transition a few months earlier, so I could not share what happened, and maybe that was a good thing. I was able to move past the assault. I was not afraid but very disturbed by this person's destructive and criminal behavior. Too bad he had not swung at Carla, one of my sisters. Dad took extra time teaching her how to box, and she would have eagerly swung back.

I decided not to tell my family because word would have gotten around to certain family members, and things would have escalated. By the way, this person had the audacity to call me a few years later for a deal. The nerve.

I love to say *Thank you*, so I would also like to take this opportunity to thank L & H Real Estate, who sponsored one hundred percent of a women's event/dinner at the large convention in Vegas in 2001. All I did was ask, and they said yes. It was an incredible event and the attendee roster included a shopping center owner, executives, brokers, and dealmakers. I wish I had a photo because many of these women were gold medalists in the industry. It was a last-minute decision to have the dinner and many of the women I called were surprised and cancelled their current dinner/meeting plans to attend. When I called, I explained the sincere interest in bringing women together. Some of them did not know me but they were pleased to hear about the dinner and eager to attend.

It may not seem like it now, but in 2001, a women's dinner with top women in the industry was a big deal at this real estate event. It was an invite-only dinner and I am told the event single-handedly advanced the careers (and wallets) of many who attended. Thank you, L & H!

I started my career at L & H, and they were such a good company, I worked there twice. After Harriett attended the L & H women's event in 2001, she said, "You should do one for African Americans." As mentioned earlier, in 2004, I was approached by two people to create a large diversity event and put it on a grand stage. This was a no-brainer. I was excited to take the event to a large scale. I called Harriett, and the four of us made history.

We are not to fear man. We are not to idolize man. A great scripture to end this chapter with follows:

You, dear children, are from God and have overcome them, because the one who is in you is greater than the one who is in the world (1 John 4:4 NIV).

CHAPTER 26
WE MEET AGAIN

"OH NO, oh no, oh no, oh no," Jamie said as she stared back at Helen and me during a Zoom call in 2020 during the global pandemic.

I turned on my ring light, positioned my camera, and we all said our hellos.

"I'm admiring her new kitchen she just completed before the country went on shutdown—or at least some of the county," I said. "A pink, red, and brown kitchen. You should have been an interior designer and not a dealmaker. You actually pulled it off.

"You would have to see it to believe it. It sounded like the clash of the kitchens when you first mentioned it, and I thought not even Martha Stewart could do it, but you did it.

"Pink and brown pots and pans, and your dishwasher turns pink when it's on…just wow," I continued.

"And the dishwasher says, 'Dish Love in Process' while it's on," Jamie said, bragging about her renovated kitchen.

"It should have said, 'Getting down and dirty.'" I laughed as I grabbed an apple from the purple-and-gold swirl-design fruit bowl on my kitchen table.

"It's your money. You give a lot away to charities, churches, and foster children, so keep enjoying yourself. God is probably blessing you so much because you give like half of your income away," Helen told Jamie.

"I enjoy giving more than spending, but seriously, guys, no, no, no, another recession," Jamie said.

"I'm so glad I have my own business. I can't imagine... Brand Sailor just laid off thousands and shuttered fourteen hundred stores. I did a deal with them. I hope they make it through," I said of the apparel company.

"Me too," Jamie replied.

"I did about seven deals with them," Helen said. "They're a solid operator, but who could survive the economy falling off a cliff that no one knew was there? One minute you're counting your homes, consecutive quarterly sales increases, and your straight-A daughter's Ivy League college acceptance letters, and the next minute, the lights turn off. The economy just…turned…off."

"Ten or so years ago, we were group hugging during the Great Recession in Madison Square Park in NYC and munching on the most divine burgers," Jamie recalled. "I knew another was coming—we all knew it—it was well overdue. But this is, I mean…ask Jesus. That's all I can say: pray, pray, and say God is my source and supply."

"Everybody—and I mean everybody, man, woman, child, pets, companies, business owners, everybody—is regrouping. It's like going on another bad date with the same guy ten years later. This time is very different. People and companies will have to change gears. Priorities will completely morph. What was hot today will be nonexistent tomorrow. Stay positive, evolve, kick fear out of your house and your head, and push your way into the room. Push your way into the next movement, the next reality because this one is over. Don't look back," I urged.

"This is so true. People keep talking about the past, I know, and I am sorry. The past was literally two months ago before the world went on lockdown, but it's the past, nonetheless. It's April 2020. The quicker we adapt, the better," Jamie said as she cleaned off her kitchen counter for the twentieth time.

"This is why I started innovative retail think tank. I've been in this industry long enough to see what's coming. This is a mass, global pivot evolution. I'm focusing on how people and companies are curating their creativity and quite literally inventing and reinventing in real time," I stated with hopeful determination. "Let's talk about regrouping of the world, life, and the industry. What are some of your favorites or shockers? I'm highlighting cool retail innovations and survival tactics. I have a call later today to share some meaty ideas with a few investors," I continued.

"Oh yes, I've been keeping up with your site. Here are some of my favorites so far…" Jamie began to rattle off her retail pivot ideas that retailers had come up with to keep sales flowing during the lockdown. Customers were not leaving their homes and had stopped buying many products that they did not need since they were staying close to and working from home.

We spent the next hour discussing retail, retail real estate, and the office and industrial real estate sectors. I then left the call to share one-of-a-kind retail evolution and survival ideas with a group of investors out of Canada.

Reader, as I typed the ending of this book, it was fall 2021, and I was a commercial real estate broker at the time. Life in commercial real estate continued to evolve. The economy had returned but not without bruising, changes, and tough lessons. It had spurned new investors, young investors, group investing, repurposing of properties, market policy changes, and more. Industrial real estate was the clear winner by a landslide followed by multifamily, and self-storage continued to storm to the top of the headlines and investors' portfolios. Investors' insatiable appetite for self-storage became a phenomenon all unto itself. Indeed, commercial real estate had roared back.

I think back to my first mentor, who hired me into the shopping center real estate industry while I was still in college and pushed me to get internship college credit for the part-time job. I am grateful this person took time to train me every day. This is unheard of today (and even back then), and it laid a good foundation for the start of my career.

I would like to thank some of the career angels who mentored me, helped me get jobs, took a chance on me, listened to my sales pitch, gave me a helping hand, or did my deal. I have listed their initials: JL, HE, DS, DH, MH, GC, PO, ML, ML, SM, CSJ, JB, MF, JB, CS, JB, JM, JB, MG. I met some amazing people in the industry who vouched for me and went the extra mile. They saw my talent, but because of ungodly stereotypes, some of them knew I would need a little extra help maneuvering in the industry and getting in the door, but make no mistake, my abilities, hard work, tenacity, and God kept me going.

Thank you, thank you, and thank you.

It has been a riveting journey thus far, and we will see what is next. Onward and upward.

Thank you, Jesus.

CHAPTER 27
OWN PROPERTY

SOIL HAS supernatural powers to bring forth life and food. It feeds a planet, and it brings beauty to the world as flowers and trees spring from it. Precious minerals and gems are born in it, and according to the Bible, we come from the earth.

According to the Bible, it is your birthright to own property/land. It is a tangible and an incredible investment when thought out and planned properly.

Isn't there something special about walking on soil you have a deed to?

Owning property should be on the top of your list. Following are scriptures from the Bible that talk about owning real estate. Select your choice scriptures, say them out loud, make a plan, and manifest, manifest, manifest.

Psalm 37:11 (NASB)

But the humble will inherit the land

And will delight themselves in abundant prosperity.

Psalm 16:6 (ESV)

The lines have fallen for me in pleasant places; indeed, I have a beautiful inheritance.

Leviticus 25:34 (NASB 1995)

But pasture fields of their cities shall not be sold, for that is their perpetual possession.

Genesis 13:17 (ESV)

Arise, walk through the length and the breadth of the land, for I will give it to you.

Deuteronomy 28:8 (ESV)

The LORD will command the blessing on you in your barns and in all that you undertake. And he will bless you in the land that the LORD your God is giving you.

Jeremiah 27:5 (ESV)

It is I who by my great power and my outstretched arm have made the earth, with the men and animals that are on the earth, and I give it to whomever it seems right to me.

Deuteronomy 19:4 (ESV)

You shall not move your neighbor's landmark, which the men of old have set, in the inheritance that you will hold in the land that the LORD your God is giving you to.

Bonus Scripture on Prosperity

Psalm 35:27 (KJV)

Let them shout for joy, and be glad, that favour my righteous cause: yea, let them say continually, Let the LORD be magnified, which hath pleasure in the prosperity of his servant.

AFTERWORD

I had to do it! I was passed the baton, and I could not fumble or fall. I had to grab it and run the race, so I am running the race of life and trying not to let it run me. I am running the race of life with my dad's playbook in tow. My dad was a Vietnam vet, championship boxer, and a self-proclaimed litigator. He was born in the 1940s and thrown into a world of war at home and abroad. He took all that he learned and endured and began to spoon-feed this knowledge and warlike survival tactics to me as young as I can remember. He raised me with purpose and the ability to protect myself.

Reality was not outside the walls. It was being fed to me regularly in my home.

His position was that the fight would come, that it was inevitable, and you had better be ready. I have war tactics and boxing strategy in my subconscious, and it is accessible to me at any moment. I see the world through a few lenses, and one of them is through the lens of an African American male born in the 1940s.

One of the greatest gifts my dad gave me was courage. I still feel this courage running through my veins today, and I take in deep breaths of it when I need to forge ahead on a decision or make major moves in my life. One of the most important things he taught me was to have no fear. This one statement made a major impact on my life and decisions.

It was an unrelenting upbringing with Dad always teaching, instilling, and reprimanding. He took all his life experiences and used them as the fuel to power my future. You went on a journey with my dad and me. You shared his strength and natural understandings of life and the puppet strings that one is always trying to break free from.

There is no way I would have survived in my current career of commercial real estate in the era I entered the industry without the boot camp upbringing I had. It is an industry where you must be both tough and diplomatic. You must be both creative and business minded. You must be a quick thinker and strategic but also have remarkable patience. And most of all, you must remain cool as a cucumber.

I had no idea when my dad was teaching me chess as a little girl how it was parallel to life. That board game with a checkered pattern and pawns and kings and queens opened my mind in an incredible way. It taught me that the most serious fights are fought with the mind and in silence.

Dad did not let me win at chess. He played skillfully and calculatedly because, after all, is this not how the game of life is played? We would sit intensely across from each other anticipating the next two, three, or four moves to keep hold of our pieces. It was a tough game but, wow, did it give me an understanding of life.

Dad took every opportunity to infuse strength, intellect, and deductive/inductive reasoning. He crammed as much in my little brain as it could handle. It would not be until I was much older that I would understand things he said and some of his actions. He essentially created a life time capsule in my brain. Everything was placed in the time capsule that I would need. He knew I would open it one day and, boy, did I. It is the gift that keeps on giving. The time capsule was so precisely formulated that there were things in it that I would not need until maybe twenty years later.

I had to do it. I looked around and knew Dad had the makings of a real fighter. My dad had a special story, and now I have finally told it, and I will always cherish the playbook he gave me.

> Dear Daddys,
>
> Your daughters need all of you. They need your presence, but they also need you to know when to remove the training wheels. They strive for your accolades, but it is your constructive criticisms that will build character. They need your hugs and your swift reprimands. They need you to run with them and to crawl with them. They need all of you. They need to know that your failures made you stronger and your wins made you strive for more. They need the small minutes in between cooking dinner and getting ready for school in the morning. Your very presence in their life is nurturing every corner of their being and shaping who they become.
>
> Dear Daddys, your daughters need all of you. Cherish the fact that God chose you to raise His children. Value your seed and show honor to the calling of being a dad.
>
> Love,
> One of your biggest fans,
> Monica

...Touch not mine anointed, And do my prophets no harm
(Psalm 105:15 KJV)

Finally, brethren, whatever things are true, whatever things are noble, whatever things are just, whatever things are pure, whatever things are lovely, whatever things are of good report, if there is any virtue and if there is anything praiseworthy—meditate on these things
(Philippians 4:8–18 KJV)

ACKNOWLEDGMENTS

I have to start out by showing my gratitude to God, who placed the blueprint of this book on my heart and mind many years ago. He was the guiding light for my pen and fingers as I typed away. I pray that You are saying, "Well *done*, thou good and faithful servant..." (Matthew 25:23 KJV).

I would like to recognize my dear friend Eric Smith. He helped inspire me to write. An English teacher and budding author, Eric explained writing like he was eating the best piece of chocolate in the world. I had to try it, and he was right. It's delicious. Thank you, Eric, for reading my first manuscript, your encouragement, guidance, and being my first cheerleader. I would also like to extend a hug and a thank you to Patricia Lytle. You believed in me, my writing, and the book, even before you read the first page. Thank you for your friendship and being one of my spiritual intercessors.

I would also like to send love and appreciation to my family for assisting in critical research.

I would like to thank David Wickenden for reading several versions of the manuscript and offering his candid, well thought out, written feedback in the early stages of editing and on several of the drafts. Thank you for pushing and cheering me on until it was published. Also appreciate you writing my first official review.

I would like to acknowledge the publishing consultant who gave me effective and laser-like guidance on being a new author and explained the publishing process. I am forever grateful for your unwavering goal to blossom new authors, being a springboard for their success. I express a sincere thank you to my editors, copy editors, and proofreaders.

A sincere thank you to Anthony V. Gentile, Esq., whose need and desire for justice is imprinted on every legal case he touches. Thank you for your advice on the chess game on the front cover. And for being one of my beta readers. Your input added additional polish and perspective. I'll remember most your phrase, "Don't hata the beta."

I am so thankful to my friends and family who took time out of their busy schedules to read the book along its journey and provide honest feedback. Thank you to my sisters Dara Ann and Carla, for making the time to read the manuscript. I must also include Jennifer Nippert. Each of you dropped everything and read the manuscript. Please know that your feedback was appreciated.

I'm extremely grateful to the book cover artist for bringing my cover idea to life. I also appreciate illustrator number two Javiere Lockett's contribution to the cover. I would also like to thank those individuals and companies who assisted in marketing my book and in research. I express a sincere appreciation to those who are in the book and are part of my story, including those named by pseudonym.

And to my younger sister, Dara Ann Smith, what fun we had producing the theme song for *Steel Victories*. *Symphony from Heaven* is a musical mirror of the book's contents. Thank you for composing and engineering my vision of a song that included jazz, Latin rhythms, house music, and other surprises. Hopefully listeners will enjoy the treasure hunt of sounds that will greet their ears.

I am thrilled you chose to spend time with me and my story. Thank you to the moon and back.

ABOUT THE AUTHOR

Monica C. Smith, a national corporate commercial real estate (CRE) director, who has managed billion-dollar portfolios, dives into the world of publishing, unleashing a hidden natural gift for writing and storytelling, which draws the reader in from the first page and never lets go.

A hard-core science fiction buff since she was a kid, Monica naturally understands the elements of storytelling and blends her vivid and imaginative writing style with her astute corporate business writing skills. This results in a captivating read, and her stories seamlessly land the literary dismount, like a gymnast who performs a perfect 10 double-double dismount on the balance beam.

Monica has closed deals in nearly all fifty states and has also walked the path of a CRE broker. A Purdue University alumna, she comes from a small city in Northwest Indiana and currently resides in the Atlanta metropolitan area. Monica is a world traveler who has also lived in New York City and Chicago. In *Steel Victories*, Monica is the ultimate tour guide. She effortlessly writes on many topics including the innocence of childhood, adult conflict, business, sports, spirituality, entertainment, and more. She proves she has writing chops and will keep the reader wanting more.

www.ingramcontent.com/pod-product-compliance
Lightning Source LLC
Chambersburg PA
CBHW030326010526
44119CB00027B/390/J